# *No Believer Left Behind*

✝

### Don Z. Weldon

CROSS BOOKS

*CrossBooks™*
*1663 Liberty Drive*
*Bloomington, IN 47403*
*www.crossbooks.com*
*Phone: 1-866-879-0502*

*Based on the original text Believers in the Hands of an Offended God. Copyright © 2003 by Thee Family. Revised 2006.*

*©2010 original No Believer Left Behind. Text for No Believer Left Behind completed 2007*

*No part of this book may be reproduced, stored in a retrieval system, or transmitted by any means without the written permission of the author.*

*First published by CrossBooks 03/23/10*

*ISBN: 978-1-6150-7067-1 (sc)*

*Library Congress of Control Number: 2009937793*

*Printed in the United States of America*
*Bloomington, Indiana*

*This book is printed on acid-free paper.*

# CONTENTS

| | |
|---|---|
| **FOREWORD** | vii |
| **NO BELIEVER LEFT BEHIND – a synopsis** | 1 |
|    EASY BELIEVISM | 4 |
|    LORDSHIP CHRISTIANITY | 5 |
|    WHAT ABOUT YOU (AND YOUR LOVED ONES)? | 25 |
| **PREFACE TO *NO BELIEVER LEFT BEHIND* - 2005** | 33 |
| **NO BELIEVER LEFT BEHIND - 2005** | 39 |
|    ETERNITY – A LONG, LONG TIME | 39 |
|    NEGLECTED SALVATION SCRIPTURES | 41 |
|    WHAT'S THE PROBLEM? | 45 |
|    PARABLE OF THE SOWER | 47 |
|    OUR LORD'S REQUIREMENTS | 48 |
|    WHO SAYS RIGHTEOUSNESS AND LORDSHIP HAVE ANYTHING TO DO WITH BEING SAVED? | 51 |
|    DOING CONVERSION WRONG | 61 |
|    NON-OPTIONAL REPENTANCE | 62 |
|    GOD'S GRACE | 65 |
|    BECOMING A NEW CREATION | 66 |
|    SPIRITUAL CYCLES | 68 |
|    BROKEN FAMILIES | 69 |
|    LEARNING AND DOING WHAT THE LORD SAYS | 70 |
|    SOME PULPIT ERRORS | 75 |

| | |
|---|---|
| SUMMARY – EASY BELIEVISM CHRISTIANITY – DOING OUR CONVERSION WRONG | 75 |
| SUMMARY – LORDSHIP CHRISTIANITY – DOING OUR CONVERSION RIGHT | 76 |
| FORSAKING EASY BELIEVISM | 78 |
| ADDING POWER TO YOUR PRAYERS | 81 |
| CONCLUSIONS | 83 |
| ALMOST PERSUADED? - 2006 | 88 |
| BELL CURVE POPULATION DISTRIBUTION | 91 |

# FOREWORD

The book is totally scripturally based and is about the problems modern Christianity is having in our society. Most Christians today are spiritually lukewarm or cold, are "overcome" by the world, thinking and acting like the world, and destroying their families and eternities like the world.

There is a major crisis regarding our generation having great difficulty rearing a godly generation because we are not a godly generation. For the most part, we are delighting in and spending our time in anything and everything other than the things of God. Church attendance is somewhat up; spirituality is down. We can do better than this and we must do better than this!

The main issue is that over the centuries there has been a destructive "evolution" in the theology of evangelism and subsequent discipling. The "early church" created spiritually "hot" Christians because they received much teaching of highly critical "new creation" preaching and letters (which became Holy Scriptures) from Matthew, John, Peter, James, Paul, Timothy, Jesus and others on the subjects of winning converts and discipling them. Evidently, through many years, overly challenged or convicted church members and possibly some leaders took action to cause these highly critical scriptures to fall into disfavor or neglect with organized religion.

For instance, during a lifetime of preaching and teaching, I have only heard one sermon on Matthew 7:21-24. I have never heard, that I can remember, anything about 7:21 since it was only read during the 21-24 message. **Matthew 7:21 Not every one that saith unto me, Lord, Lord, shall enter into the kingdom of heaven; but he that doeth the will of my Father which is in heaven.** It is incredibly amazing that intensely loving God and others (#1 and #2 commands) is not typically any part of the terminology, understanding, and commitments to decide to become a Christian. I don't believe I ever heard that Paul instructs us to become "servants of righteousness" (Romans 6:18)! Ninety nine percent of the times I heard Ephesians 2:8-9 frequently mentioned in sermons, the all important verse 10 was omitted.

These and many other scriptures that fell away, were ignored or misinterpreted will be thoroughly discussed in No Believer Left Behind and take their rightful place in Christian dialogue.

Do not be fearful of this material because it is somewhat different from what you are familiar with. It is not something new and modern. It is taking what most people are familiar with and putting back in what was ignored or misinterpreted many years ago that mostly ruined the truth of the Bible for many people and their eternal destinies. This material is dominated with scriptures, backed with tragic modern circumstances, supported with surveys and has survived the scrutiny of several theological "big guns"!

<u>No Believer Left Behind</u> can also lead non-believers to a genuine born again Lordship relationship with the Lord (God the Father, God the Son, and God the Holy Spirit). Additionally, if a family is mildly struggling, in serious deterioration, or in major demolition mode, we have found that when Lordship comes to the family, miracles happen! What incredible life-changing power you have from God when you get your heart and soul (your spirit) in right, loving, indwelling relationship with Him! **2 Chron. 16:9 For the eyes of the Lord run to and fro throughout the whole earth to shew himself strong in the behalf of them whose heart is perfect toward him. 2 Cor. 5:17 Therefore if any man be in Christ, he is a new creature: old things are passed away; behold, all things are become new.**

# NO BELIEVER LEFT BEHIND – a synopsis

Attached is a list of scriptures. The first three scriptures on page 4 encompass the <u>main</u> emphasis of an "Easy Believism" request for salvation and subsequent discipleship. The remaining scriptures are <u>some</u> of the key scriptures related to "Lordship Christianity".

Lordship Christianity can't take place without the wonderful, non-optional Easy Believism scriptures being embraced! However, Lordship Christianity adds a few extremely relevant Lordship scriptures to the process and decision to become saved such that the convert has more understanding, commitment and motivation to develop a genuine relationship with Jesus Christ and God and become a true follower of Him and His Word.

This is not changing the gospel message. This is reinstalling or re-emphasizing some scriptures highly relevant to salvation that were originally written into the gospel, but evidently fell out of favor and focus as fallen man's "gospel" theology evolved through the centuries. It is dramatically increasing the marvelous power of a genuine faith and relationship with the Lord by including some extremely relevant biblical principles into evangelism and discipling that evidently should never have been neglected (or was never included in some men's interpretation of what should be the contents of the "good news" of the gospel in the first place even though these scriptures were in the Bible.)

One of the most desperate needs of "Christians" is the 100% assurance they are saved and that they will go to heaven. A recent survey of Christians revealed that only 55% of those who identified themselves as "born again Christians" feel that they have 100% assurance that they are going to heaven. "Born again" is a term typically identifying those who are the "most spiritual" of those professing faith in the Lord and calling on Him to save them.

A highly critical question to anyone who is concerned with leading people to become saved and discipling them to grow in the Lord is this: "**IN LIGHT OF THE LORDSHIP SCRIPTURES, can we, with complete <u>scriptural</u> honesty, integrity and credibility tell them that they have a 100% assurance of heaven if they say that they believe in the Lord and call on the Lord for salvation without their desire, intention, and growing success of having in their heart and soul an indwelling, repentant, obedience/love relationship with the Lord?**"

When we focus on the Lordship scriptures, it seems very scripturally appropriate to say that for the minority of church members who get into Lordship Christianity, the answer is "yes", there is 100% assurance. For the majority who seemingly <u>get stuck at Easy Believism</u>, (do not become genuine obedient followers of the Lord), the answer is possibly between "maybe" and "probably not". These spiritually disillusioned souls soon find that their "faith" is not working for them. They most likely will have continued destructive sin habits, lack of love, joy, or peace, struggling with an angry or bitter spirit, broken relationships, living in defeat with little self-control, and yielding to temptations. Answers to prayer, seeing unusual blessings from God and spiritual excitement about a personal relationship with the Lord and obedience to His Word, seems foreign to them. They stay or become spiritually lukewarm or cold and drop out of church (or stay in the church) all the while thinking that they are hopefully saved. They become victims of being "overcome by the world" (a condition contrary to [true] believers in 1 John 5:1-5). If our stubborn self-will, which the Lord will not override, refuses to genuinely "open the door" and let Him in (His Spirit) to abide or indwell, and affect our lives within His will, ways and words, the confession and request for salvation becomes meaningless. This greatly prohibits our ability to have a saving relationship with Jesus Christ. (Rev. 3:1-6, 14-21, Matt. 7:21 and many other Lordship scriptures.)

Earnestly pray as you study the Lordship scriptures and see if this rings true in your mind and spirit.

There is a host of problems in our individuals, churches, families and society that can be directly attributed to church members who express belief and requests for salvation but do not become true followers of the Lord (easy believism).

Five of the greatest consequences are:

* Some very highly visible evangelists and a broad scale survey of pastors reveal they feel that between 50% and 80% of those who think they are saved, are not.

* Surveys reveal that we are losing 85% of the youth of our churches "to the world" by age 26.

* The divorce rate inside the church memberships are just as great as the general population.

* A recent survey reveals that only nine percent of "Christians" in America think and govern their lives in obedience to the holy standards of the Bible. Many potential converts are turned off to Christianity by offensive thinking, attitudes and ungodly behavior (and influence) by "Christians." In many people, much of their motivation to render Christianity illegal or destroy it comes from this.

* Ninety percent of Christians feel they have no personal relationship with Jesus Christ.

We must learn how to avoid creating new potentially "lost" church members and help the "old" lost church members realize who they are and to become genuinely saved. What an incredible field that is ripe unto harvest.

Most indicators point to easy believism evangelism and discipling theology as being the major contributor of "unsaved" church members.

## EASY BELIEVISM

### John 3:16

> For God so loved the world, that he gave his only begotten Son, that whosoever believeth in him should not perish, but have everlasting life.

### Romans 10:13

> For whosoever shall call upon the name of the Lord shall be saved.

### 1 John 1:9

> If we confess our sins, he is faithful and just to forgive us our sins, and to cleanse us from all unrighteousness.

In easy believism, stated faith and belief in His name, blood sacrifice, death, burial and resurrection may or may not cancel all our past, present and future sins. To many easy believism "converts", becoming a genuine born again "new creation" obedient follower of Jesus Christ and His ways and words is generally taught but considered <u>optional</u> as far as being saved is concerned. The minority of easy believism converts grow into obedient followers of Jesus; the vast majority evidently does not.

# LORDSHIP CHRISTIANITY

## John 3:16-21

[16] For God so loved the world, that he gave his only begotten Son, that whosoever believeth in him should not perish, but have everlasting life. [17] For God sent not his Son into the world to condemn the world; but that the world through him might be saved. [18] He that believeth on him is <u>not condemned</u>: **but he** that believeth not is condemned already, because he hath not believed in the name of the only begotten Son of God. [19] And this is the <u>condemnation</u>, that light is come into the world, and men loved darkness rather than light, because their deeds were evil. [20] For every one that doeth evil hateth the light, neither cometh to the light, lest his deeds should be reproved. [21] **But he** that doeth truth cometh to the light, that his deeds may be made manifest, that they are <u>wrought in God</u>.

These scriptures and observable circumstances indicate that there can be two types of "believers" – <u>a condemned one</u> who states or prays that he "believes" but continues to love and live in darkness, and to stay his old carnal self, refusing to come to JESUS and live His "light" (truth). He may believe that Jesus is the Son of God with his mind but in his heart he refuses to respond appropriately to what Jesus, the Son of God, has come to do to and for his soul and life!

## John 3:36

He that believeth on the Son hath everlasting life: and he that believeth not [**does not** <u>obey*</u>] the Son shall not see life; but the wrath of God abideth on him.

*Original language in <u>this verse</u> (Strong's Exhaustive Concordance of the KJV, Revised Standard, Today's English, New English Bible and English Standard Versions of the Bible)

**Truly believing in Jesus and calling on Him to save us must translate into obeying His teachings (Word) and promptings.** If we believe that Jesus is God the Son (along with God the Father, and God the Holy Spirit – the trinity), then He too is the creator and controller of everything including us who truly believe in Him. We are not His followers (John 10:25-28) if we do not respond in obedience to Jesus as **our** lord, master, controller, king or supreme authority.

With easy believism we can pray and call on the Lord to be our savior from hell and take us to Heaven and miss being His. The Lord knows those who are His (2 Tim. 2:19). In Lordship if we believe and call on Him as savior <u>and Lord</u> (our supreme authority to whom we are obedient), then we become His!

Salvation is a work of the Lord and His magnificent gifts of grace and blood sacrifice. Nothing we can do can earn our salvation. However, if we respond appropriately to God's gift and truly become saved with Jesus as <u>OUR LORD</u> – we will find ourselves increasingly performing God's will – all sorts of righteous thinking, attitudes and acts He requires of us and that please Him.

In John 3:21(and note the first phrase of verse 18 above and the two but he's), a <u>non-condemned</u> Believer is one who is prompted by the Holy Spirit and believes and is attracted to and comes to Jesus and His light. It is obvious (to others) that he lives his life in a way that indicates that his spirit and behavior are in obedience <u>cooperating with the Lord's Spirit in him</u> (original language, i.e. it is apparent his deeds are influenced by his relationship with God in that they are "wrought" in God). This is how Jesus defines a Believer!

We find some parallel meaning in I John 5:4,5 where we find a description of what happens to a true Believer. John 3:19,20 above defines <u>a condemned person</u> as someone who "believes" in Jesus but rejects His light and truth, remains in darkness, and is <u>"overcome" by the world</u>. John 3:21 describes a <u>non-condemned believer</u> who comes to Jesus' light (commands, teachings), lives it, and <u>overcomes the world</u>.

## 1 John 1:8

> If we say that we have no sin, we deceive ourselves, and the truth is not in us.

## 1 John 1:10

If we say that we have not sinned, we make him a liar, and his word is not in us.

## 1 John 3:5-9

And ye know that he was manifested **("appeared"** in the original language) to take away our sins; and in him is no sin. [6] Whosoever abideth in him sinneth not: whosoever sinneth hath not seen him, neither known him. [7] Little children, let no man deceive you: he that doeth righteousness is righteous, even as he is righteous. [8] He that committeth sin is of the devil; for the devil sinneth from the beginning. For this purpose the Son of God was manifested **(appeared)**, that he might destroy the works of the devil. [9] Whosoever is born of God doth not commit sin; for his seed remaineth in him: and he cannot sin, because he is born of God.

Jesus did not come to earth just to forgive us and save us from our sins. He came to save us from sinning too. We will not become sinless but we will sin less and less with Him as our <u>Lord and Master</u> NOW, not just as our savior in the FUTURE! (See Heb. 10:25-31 – note that Paul is writing to church members.)

God does not change and has not changed. From Genesis to Revelation He requires obedience to His Word by those who are His. The coming of Jesus did not change this (Matt. 5,6,7, especially 5:12-20, &:21).

With the Lord being our personal Lord, we have a whole new way of thinking and acting as we sin less and less!

Let's look at the "love" standard that God and Jesus brought to earth. The Lord loves you dearly. Before Jesus came to earth, people, including those professing to be God's people, were very cruel in many ways to each other. Roman bondage and treatment was awful. Evidently family relationships had not improved (see last scripture in the Old Testament and Luke 1:16-17). The society at that time that would crucify the Son of God would be more than somewhat short on mercy, compassion, spiritual understanding and scriptural reasoning. Perhaps

Roman bondage and Pharisee legalism were parts of the curse promised by God.

Christ not only displays His love and concern for you by dying for your sins but also to reduce or stop other people and followers of His from sinning against you (and you against them). The Lord strongly teaches, insists or commands others not to harm you and your family in any way, - not to murder or physically abuse you, not steal from you, or lie, deceive, mistreat, or take advantage of you, neglect, or gossip about you, envy or desire your wife, children, or possessions. They are not to hate you, seduce your mate, break up your family or cause your children to stumble, nor are they even to have a prideful, haughty spirit or exclusionary attitude around you, take revenge against you, or cheat you in business.

In fact, if you are hungry, thirsty or need clothing, they are to serve you, to help you. In a sense the Lord keeps non-followers of His from harming you because many of the laws of society came from His teachings.

These are just a few of the commands and teachings wrapped up in the number two commandment of Jesus, "Love others as yourself." The first commandment of the Lord is to INTENSELY LOVE Him, which meaningfully connects these teachings with the scripture that if we love Him we will keep His commandments (John 14:21, 23). Also, we cannot legitimately call Him "Lord" if we do not do what He says (Luke 6:46). Those who do not love others and who treat them badly or negligently are not genuine followers (1 John 3:10).

Jesus is very, very serious about His followers loving and meeting the needs of others, and them not sinning against others He loves. (For example see Matt. 25:31-46, note #34, 41 & 46.) Doing these things in these scriptures in our own strength will not save us. However, if we are genuine followers of the Lord, intensely loving Him and others, He will lead us and enable us to do these and many other acts of righteousness indicating a saving relationship with Him!

In Lordship Christianity, faith and belief in His name, blood sacrifice, death, burial and resurrection cancels all our past, present and future sins. In Lordship Christianity, becoming a "born again" obedient follower of Jesus and His ways and words <u>are not optional</u>.

### Romans 10:9

> That if thou shalt confess with thy mouth the <u>Lord</u> Jesus, and shalt believe in thine heart that God hath raised him from the dead, thou shalt be saved.

### Romans 10:13

> For whosoever shall call upon the name of the <u>Lord</u> shall be saved.

The original language meaning of "Lord" <u>in the above scriptures</u> is this: as we believe on Him, it is necessary to "call" on Him not as <u>the</u> Lord but as <u>OUR PERSONAL LORD</u> (master, king, sovereign authority, or controller). Then we will be saved.

### 1 John 1:9

> If we confess our sins, he is faithful and just to forgive us our sins, and to cleanse us from all unrighteousness.

Easy believism embraces and uses this scripture out of context. In **many** scriptures in 1 John and on both sides of this verse are numerous instructions to obey Jesus (walk in His light and keep His commandments.) If our heart, spirit and life are in relative harmony with Jesus, and we confess and repent of our sins, then we will be cleansed from all unrighteousness (see 1 John 1:7). If we confess a sin and intentionally, continually or habitually keep repeating it for the rest or most of our lives, the confession is meaningless (Hebrews 10:26-31). Genuinely repenting, overcoming and obeying Jesus' teachings are the ways to be cleansed from unrighteousness and grow in righteousness.

Incidentally, the Lord did not say He would separate the sins from the sinner as far as the east is from the west in the easy believism hypocritical, superficial, self-willed and non-genuine followers of Him. **He will**, however, if we have a healthy **fear of the Lord, keep His covenant and follow His commandments.** Then we will obtain His pity, mercy and receive His removal of these transgressions. (Ps 103, 11-13, 17-18).

The above scriptural interpretations are strongly supported by the following partial list of Lordship scriptures.

## 2 Peter 1:5

> And beside this, giving all diligence, <u>ADD TO YOUR FAITH</u> virtue; and to virtue knowledge; *(and other non-optional righteous qualities including the all important quality - LOVE)*

## 2 Peter 1:10-11

> Wherefore the rather, brethren, give diligence to <u>make your calling and election sure</u>: for if ye do these things *(adding righteous qualities to faith)*, ye shall never fall: [11] <u>For so an entrance shall be ministered unto you abundantly into the everlasting kingdom of our Lord and Saviour Jesus Christ.</u>

## Ephes. 2:8-10

> **For by grace are ye saved through faith**; and that not of yourselves: it is the gift of God: [9] Not of works, lest any man should boast. [10] **For we are his workmanship, created in Christ Jesus unto good works, which God hath before ordained that we should walk in them.**

Paul, in vs. 10 above sounds really close to what Peter is saying above (2 Peter 1:5) when he, Paul, states we are to become and live Christ's righteousness that we receive through God's gift of grace. This is very parallel to what Paul is saying in Romans 6:18 that we are to <u>become servants of righteousness</u>, and what James is saying in 2:26 that faith without works (obviously good works) is dead, and Jesus says in John 3:21 that a true Believer's acts indicate that Jesus' light and truth (righteousness) are in him. In the Sermon on the Mount and the Ten Commandments, the Lord is saying, "Add righteousness (and turn from unrighteousness) to your faith. Most of the Bible is trying to convince and motivate us to become righteous and live righteous lives according to our Lord's teachings. **ADDING RIGHTEOUSNESS TO OUR FAITH MUST COME THROUGH A POWERFUL, INTIMATE**

**PRESENCE OF JESUS AND HIS LOVE IN US OR IT WILL BECOME AN ATTEMPT AT HUMAN EFFORT "SALVATION BY WORKS"AND WHAT SOME PEOPLE CALL "LEGALISM".**

Note that one way or another in all these Lordship Christianity scriptures, it is indicated that **through a strong loving, abiding relationship with Jesus**, adding righteousness and/or eliminating unrighteousness are necessary parts of our faith and belief in our Lord and Master.

Unfortunately, in "easy believism", to many it seems that <u>adding righteous deeds</u>, living in obedience to His commandments and greatly reducing sin are considered optional or unnecessary parts of our faith and belief and have very little to do with going to heaven.

<u>Simply put, adding more and more of the presence, power, and wisdom of the Spirit of Jesus and His righteousness to our faith is the goal of the discipling process.</u> However, when many of us make the initial decision to become an easy believism "Christian", we are willing to casually endure and tolerate the <u>discipling process</u> for a lifetime of preaching, teaching and possibly self study. However, our fallen nature can lead us to refuse to embrace and live a righteous life according to scripture. (See 2 Timothy 3:1-8, especially note in verses 7 and 8 that Paul is writing about those in the household of faith!).

Many of us are told just to verbalize our belief and ask to be saved (no matter how superficial) and <u>this does it all</u> as far as our becoming saved as a Christian and achieving our objectives of going to heaven. Some of us have been told <u>that does it all </u>no matter what we say, think, do, or become afterwards and these cannot become too bad! This will not stand up under Lordship Christianity. For examples, pray and meditate on 1 John.

Paul's Romans 4-6 continuing discussion of imputed righteousness (Ro. 4:8, 22, 23) eventually translates into a person "dieing to sin" and becoming a "servant of righteousness" (Ro. 6:12,14,18). This whole process in a Believer must be laced with much Jesus-inspired and empowered obedience to His holy requirements.

This <u>No Believer Left Behind</u> material is not about someone losing their salvation. It is about easy believism allowing many "converts" to live in hyper-carnality and evidently never be saved in the first place. Nor is it "salvation by works" or "legalism". Christ inspired and orchestrated obedience to the Lord's Word is not "legalism"!

It is only carnally natural for many of us to want to postpone embracing the discipling principles until we are old, or we consider these principles to be unnecessary options.

## Matthew 28:20  (Part of the Great Commission of Jesus)

Teaching them *(new converts)* <u>to observe (*hold fast, keep*) all things whatsoever I have commanded you</u>: and, lo, I am with you alway, even unto the end of the world. Amen.

## Matthew 22:36-39

Master, which is the great commandment in the law? [37] Jesus said unto him, Thou shalt love the Lord thy God with all thy heart, and with all thy soul, and with all thy mind. [38] <u>This is the first and great commandment</u>. [39] And the second is like unto it, Thou shalt love thy neighbour as thyself. (Greatly focus on John 14:21 below).

## John 14:21

He that hath my commandments, <u>and keepeth them, he it is that loveth me</u>: ….

## 1 John 2:4

He that saith, <u>I know him, and keepeth not his commandments, is a liar</u>, and <u>the truth is not in him.</u>

## Luke 10:25-28

And, behold, a certain lawyer stood up, and tempted him, saying, Master, **what shall I do to inherit eternal life**? [26] He said unto him, What is written in the law? how readest thou? [27] And he answering said, Thou shalt love the Lord thy God with all thy heart, and with all thy soul, and with all thy strength, and with all thy mind; and thy neighbour as thyself. [28] And he said unto him, Thou hast answered right: this do, and thou shalt live.

*(With certainty, this indicates that intensely loving the Lord and others should be a critical understanding in the decision and commitments when "calling on the Lord to be saved" expecting admittance to heaven. These #1 and #2 commands of the Lord are not optional in evangelism or discipleship or our relationship with Him.)*

## John 14:21-23

<u>He that hath my commandments, and keepeth them, he it is that loveth me</u>: and he that loveth me shall be loved of my Father, and I will love him, <u>and will manifest myself to him</u>. [22] Judas saith unto him, not Iscariot, Lord, how is it that thou wilt manifest thyself unto us, and not unto the world? [23] Jesus answered and said unto him, <u>If a man love me, he will keep my words: and my Father will love him, and we will come unto him</u>, and make our abode with him.

The indelible way to add righteous qualities to your faith and belief is to love the Lord intensely and others and to make absolutely sure that you let Him and His ways in when you asked Him in (wholeheartedly "opening the door" Rev. 3:20). When we genuinely let Him in, <u>He brings His righteousness with Him</u>. This plus loving Him and learning of His righteousness gives us <u>power</u> to do His teachings! "Thy word have I hid in mine heart, that I might not sin against thee." (Psalm 119:11)

## Psalm 145:18-20

The Lord is nigh unto all them that call upon him, to all that <u>CALL UPON HIM IN TRUTH</u>. [19] <u>He will fulfil the desire of them that fear him</u>: he also will hear their cry, and will <u>save them</u>. [20] <u>The Lord preserveth all them that love him: but all the wicked will he destroy.</u>

## 2 Tim. 2:19

Nevertheless the foundation of God standeth sure, having this seal, <u>THE LORD KNOWETH THEM THAT ARE HIS.</u> And,

Don Z. Weldon

> Let <u>EVERY ONE THAT NAMETH THE NAME OF CHRIST DEPART FROM INIQUITY</u> (self-serving sin).

## 1 John 4:15

> [15] Whosoever shall confess that Jesus is the Son of God, <u>God dwelleth in him, and he in God.</u>

If we confess that Jesus is God's Son, that means to us He is our Lord too. If He is God, along with God (part of the Trinity – God the Father, God the Son, and God the Holy Spirit), He is also the indwelling, abiding Lord, Master, King and supreme authority over everything, including us doing the confessing that Jesus is the Son of God.

## Romans 8:9

> But ye are not in the flesh, but in the Spirit, if so be that the <u>Spirit of God dwell in you.</u> <u>Now if any man have not the Spirit of Christ, he is none of his.</u>

## Matthew 7:21

> Not every one that saith unto me, Lord, Lord, shall enter into the kingdom of heaven; <u>but he that doeth the will of my Father</u> which is in heaven.

What is the will of God? It is much more than just the big items of our life – who we marry, how we make our living, where we live, whether we serve in a ministry etc. It is hearing, learning and doing what He says (adding righteousness to our faith and reducing self-will unrighteousness) to faith and belief. <u>Truly following Him</u> is the solution to keep from being told, "Depart from Me… (Matt. 7:23, 24. The word "therefore" is the key. Also, some beautiful examples of some of God's will are found in Rom. 12:1, 2, 9-21)

## Luke 6:46-47

> **And why call ye me, Lord, Lord, and do not the things which I say?** [47] Whosoever <u>cometh to me</u>, and <u>heareth my sayings, and doeth them,</u> I will shew you to whom he is like:

If we do not do what Jesus says (obedience) we cannot legitimately call Him our "Lord".

## Luke 13:3

I tell you, Nay: but, EXCEPT YE REPENT, YE SHALL ALL LIKEWISE PERISH.

Repenting goes beyond becoming aware of our sin, feeling sorry for our sin. It is confessing and intentionally forsaking and overcoming the sin. A relationship with Jesus and the presence of His Holy Spirit in our lives empowers us to do this (Ro. 7:18-8:1-11).

## Acts 17:30

And the times of this ignorance God winked at; but now commandeth all men every where to repent:

## Galatians 5:24

And THEY THAT ARE CHRIST'S HAVE CRUCIFIED THE FLESH with the affections and lusts.

(an example of turning and repenting from unrighteousness and thereby adding righteousness to faith).

## Romans 6:18

Being then made FREE FROM SIN, YE BECAME THE SERVANTS OF RIGHTEOUSNESS *(adding righteousness to faith and belief)*

## 1 John 5:4-5

For whatsoever is born of God overcometh the world: and this is the victory that overcometh the world, even our faith. [5] Who is he that overcometh the world, but he that believeth that Jesus is the Son of God?

Summary of 1 John 5:1-5. Only those who truly believe in, love, and embrace the Lord (as their Master), and His Light are able to keep His commandments and have the power to overcome the temptations and destructions of the world.

## Romans 1:21-22

> Because that, <u>when they knew God, they glorified him not as God</u>, neither were thankful; but became vain in their imaginations, and their foolish heart was darkened. [22] Professing themselves to be wise, they became fools,

Knowing God (and just saying or praying we believe or even really believe in Him) **but not glorifying Him as our personal Lord and Master** leaves us wide open to Satan's persuasions, foolish thinking, void of self-control and other fruit of the Spirit (Gal. 5:22), living in darkness and easily being overcome by the world! Psalm 14:1 states that a fool says in his heart that there is no God. Romans 1:21, 22 strongly suggests that a person who says, "**No**! God, you are God, but you can't be **My God** to whom I'm obedient," becomes a fool!

## Titus 1:16

> They profess that they know God; but in works they deny him, being abominable, and disobedient, and unto every good work reprobate.

## 1 John 3:10

> In this the children of God are manifest, and the children of the devil: whosoever doeth not righteousness is not of God, neither he that loveth not his brother.

## 2 Cor. 5:17

> Therefore **if any man be in Christ,** <u>he is a new creature: old things are passed away; behold, all things are become new</u> *(adding righteous obedience, reducing disobedience).*

Throughout the "No Believer Left Behind" material you will find that it is imperative that in the initial conversion decision and request to be saved, there must be at least some understanding (through scriptures), that a person's heart and soul must intend to have an abiding, (Rom. 8:9, John 15:5, 1 John 4:15) repenting, overcoming, (Luke 13:3, also see Rev. 2 & 3) and obedience/love (Matt. 28:20, John 14:21) relationship with the Lord.

*No Believer Left Behind*

To better predispose the new Believer into becoming a true God-pleasing saved follower of the Lord, let's consider at least putting some of these and/or other related scriptures into the initial decision process to become a Christian.

As we have emphasized over and over, to make the <u>conversion decision</u> based primarily upon faith and belief without some understanding and commitment as to the necessity of obedience to the Lord is lifetime and eternally lethal for many "converts". How crucial the hymn: "<u>Trust and Obey</u>", for there's is no other way"!

This is not totally in sync with childhood conversion. However, down the road the growing up child or adult must become aware and develop this type of relationship with the Lord or they will stay or become spiritually cold or lukewarm and be overcome by the world. They will become prime targets for Satan's schemes to destroy them, their families, their lives and their futures. This is incredibly confirmed by the <u>unbelievable</u> divorce statistics of church members!

Circumstances and surveys seem to indicate that in most congregations when the majority of the members hear or read the "words of the Kingdom", their minds, hearts and spirits are in rigid groups of hard packed, rocky or thorny "soil conditions" producing lukewarm, cold, continual workers of iniquity. It is extremely difficult for preaching and teaching to move the members toward becoming "new creations". They will be greatly facilitated in doing this as Lordship Christianity preaching can prepare and motivate resistant soil into becoming "good soil", yielding much fruit (righteous qualities and deeds – Matt. 13:1-23).

All this emphasis on doing what the Lord says is not by any means "salvation by works"! Becoming and doing righteousness will not save us. **A GENUINE FAITH, INTIMATE ABIDING LOVE/ OBEDIENCE RELATIONSHIP WITH JESUS WILL!** If we have this kind of relationship with Jesus Christ, we will find ourselves having His motivation and His power, doing all sorts of righteousness and eliminating all sorts of unrighteousness. (Luke 6:46-47, Gal. 5:24, Rom. 6:18)

It seems that many religious leaders feel that because they were able to grow and progress <u>into a Lordship relationship</u> from initially <u>believing in</u> and <u>asking the Lord for salvation</u>, others ought to be able to do likewise. Obviously, many indicators in our society and churches show that some do, most do not! There are horrible tragedies now. The worst tragedies in the history of the universe are lining up at the end times. Just imagine the shock, grieving and wailing when those spiritually cold, and lukewarm disobedient "Believers" who thought they were saved may hear, "Depart from Me" or "I'm going to spit you out of my mouth" (Matt. 7:21-24, Rev. 3:15 & 16, Luke 13:23, 24, 27, 28). These scriptures seem far from being welcome mats into Heaven for disobedient and lukewarm "believers". The Lordship scriptures indicate this can and probably will happen. **PUTTING ALL OUR SALVATION AND HEAVEN STOCK INTO A POSSIBLE SUPERFICIAL EASY BELIEVISM "CONVERSION" SEEMS TO BE A TRAGIC GAMBLE WHEN OUR FOREVER AND FOREVER ETERNITY IS AT STAKE.**

All this can sound harsh and uncomfortable but if America is to spiritually wake up before it is too late, we must come to grips with some of these very challenging scriptures that are in the Bible just as are the more easy to embrace comfortable passages. Ignoring these has gotten us into some deep trouble.

If we make some adjustments to include them with the Lord's guidance and power while living our lives and worshiping the Lord, very positive benefits will come to our individuals, families, churches and nation. There will be great decreases in affairs and divorce, great enhancements in reproducing Godly generations, great increases in those going into heaven, and great improvements in our standing and position with the Lord to be a God-blessed and protected nation! (2 Chron. 7:14)

If the statistic is accurate that taking away military expenditures, sixty percent of the national budget goes to pay for the cost of individuals violating Biblical standards, think of how much more funding would be available for more noble and righteous causes.

Many religious leaders of our day are becoming aware of how much trouble we are in because of "easy believism" (Some call this <u>easy</u>

grace; others call it <u>superficial profession</u>, and others call it <u>counterfeit Christianity</u>). The faster we transition into Lordship evangelism and discipleship the better!

The following was taken from a 2007 Bible study guide of a major denomination.

> ..."When a person is drawn by the Spirit through the gospel to <u>believe</u> in Jesus and **responds affirmatively**, the <u>Holy Spirit</u> comes to <u>take up residence in that believer</u>. The Spirit works to <u>purify and change</u> the individual, producing the <u>fruit of Christ-like living within the believer</u>. The Spirit then draws the believer into a <u>close, obedient walk with the Lord Jesus</u>. He does this through <u>His inner witness</u> in the individual, through <u>consistent Bible reading and prayer</u>, through <u>fellowship</u> and <u>worshiping with other believers</u>, and many other means of spiritual development."

This is what Lordship Christianity is intending to do for everyone going through a profession of faith and spiritual growth. As we discussed earlier, currently the above has worked for the minority of those making professions but not for the majority.

Lordship Christianity would emphasize the meaning of "responds affirmatively" (two paragraphs up), would involve the person being <u>attracted to the truth and light of Jesus</u>, wholeheartedly <u>inviting Him in and opening the door for Him and His Light to come in as Master</u>, being aware of the necessity of intensely loving Him and others whom Jesus loves too (Matt. 25:44-46), and understanding the requirement to be able to "repent and overcome" and be and do what the Lord says.

From this kind of relationship with Jesus, the Holy Spirit can do the work in the new Believer defined above. This gives the Believer inner desire and power he would not otherwise have.

For years if the churches of America would have had these non-denominational LORDSHIP scriptures as an underpinning of all persuasions of decisions to becoming a Christian and growing as a Christian, what an incredibly different society we would have, and how much more united the nation, unified the churches (within and interdenominationally) and more secure would be homes and the eternal destinies of those making professions of faith! How much more secure would be the survival of our nation as provided by Almighty God! Throughout His story, (history) He has destroyed societies forsaking Him and His ways.

Surveys and circumstances indicate that America has fallen into such a desperate spiritual condition that our churches must become houses of **righteous pray**ers whose prayers "availeth much". (Matt. 21:13, Ja. 5:15)

We need a revival but a revival that far exceeds those of history which have been temporary. We do not know how long Jesus will tarry. He may come soon or wait longer. In the meantime, we desperately need as long as necessary for a revival based upon a major spiritual visitation and awakening. (2 Peter 3:10-14)

The Lord does not change and neither does His Word. Our needed spiritual awakening must not waver from the straight and narrow of the Bible. Lordship Christianity does this!

Consider this – Two of the fastest growing religions in America grow because they have an "asset" that affects behavior that most of the main stream church theologies have not recently emphasized. They have to obey their teachings if they want their ultimate reward – their heaven.

From some very limited observations and inquiries, it seems that their religions generally work for them in some important areas. Three examples would be that their families are generally strong, they ordinarily obey their moral standards, and their children typically follow in their footsteps.

Lordship Christianity provides a similar "asset" in a free-will indirect way. In easy believism we do not have to obey our Lord's teachings.

However, **if we establish a Lordship relationship with our Lord, our wills and His will merge with each other which inspires and empowers us to obey His teachings!** This Lordship love/obedience repentant relationship will provide many earthly rewards including strong families, high moral standards, successfully passing this on to future generations, and it will enable us to achieve our ultimate reward – heaven.

This No Believer Left Behind material took seven years of off and on hard labor – hundreds of hours of prayer, studying reference Bibles (non-commentary), an eight translation New Testament, and a Strong's Exhaustive Concordance.

We wanted to learn God's answers (not men's) as to why "Christians" and churches in America are having so many problems and what the scriptural solutions are. Surprisingly, after finishing the No Believer Left Behind material and revealing the project to a spiritual authority, I learned an extremely similar book was written in 1988 by one of America's foremost authors and pastors. At first I was somewhat disheartened, but as I read this book loaned to me by the pastor, I became very encouraged. This book confirmed my strong convictions that Lordship Christianity was just what our nation of "believers" needs and that our various theologies since 1988 have not yet embraced the Lordship theology to the extent necessary. It seems obvious that God wants Lordship revisited **to a much greater extent**. American Christianity currently has many more massive problems and enemies than were present in 1988. Maybe now we will be more receptive.

I hope you see my heart in this material that the above scenario is accurate. Deceiving others goes against what this material is about. Also, such deception would insure that the Lord would not bless the desired outcome of the material. Deceiving, especially leaders, does not track well with the holy requirements of our Lord. See Acts 5:1-11 for the account of Ananias and Sapphira.

As a nation of 80% professed Christians, let's strongly consider getting into <u>Lordship Christianity</u>. The traditional and modern theologies and strategies for reaching the lost and discipling them **have had their time in the sun**. Circumstances and the Holy Scriptures indicate that we must do better; we can do better!

With the predominance of easy believism conversions, the vast majority of my generation seemingly felt there was a cloud of fog around what we <u>were supposed to do about sin</u> after we "accepted Jesus as our Savior". We felt we had a whole lifetime to accomplish any self determined degree of spiritual growth, so we subconsciously ignored or pushed that process back until we would become old or near death. Meanwhile any sinning, no matter how bad, was all taken care of by the Lord with or without any confessing or repentance taking place. Obedience to parents was fairly strict; obedience to the Lord seemed optional.

Loving the Lord with all our hearts and loving others as ourselves, Jesus' Spirit indwelling us and empowering us, and obedience to the Lord's teaching, our having a personal relationship with Jesus and repenting were evidently so seldom mentioned that it did not seem to have any bearing on our thinking, attitudes, behavior or future with the Lord. Therefore most of us lived a vast array of behaviors from mild rebellion to hyper carnality.

Without the Lordship scriptures and principles being part of our faith, when our spiritual leaders tried to motivate us to witness, tithe, serve others, behave, attend regularly, or grow spiritually it was described as being as difficult as herding cats or pushing a chain uphill! It seems that perhaps much of this is still going on.

We had very little inclination or motivation to learn and obey the Lord's teachings and live in righteousness since we felt our ultimate reward of going to heaven was already taken care of by us simply saying or praying, "I believe. Come into my heart Lord Jesus," no matter how genuine or insincere we were in the statements. Of most importance to most of us was remaining "our own boss" and looking, thinking and acting in compromise or compliance to our world resulting in our being overcome by the world.

If a parent expects their children to be disobedient or rebellious, and becomes resigned to thinking they can't do any better, generally that is what they become. If the parents expect and treat their children as if they are to be compliant to their teachings, (and continually establish <u>the Lord</u> as <u>their Lord</u>, and rely on Him to help them keep "winning the children's hearts) then most likely they will peacefully and obediently pass through the rebellious years. There are many parallels between the parent/child relationship and the Lord/Christian relationship.

We must reconsider the way God feels about our continuing to live in darkness after we become "saved". Easy believism says it's okay. We're "dirty rotten helpless sinners saved by grace" and it is an option to stay that way. Lordship Christianity says we can and must do better. With Jesus' Spirit, power and love in us, we can repent, overcome the world, and increasingly live in obedience to the Lord's righteousness because we're saved by grace (Eph. 2:8-10). Many Lordship scriptures demonstrate beyond a shadow of a doubt that the Lord expects and requires increasing compliance to His will and ways (commandments and teachings) if we are HIS. The rewards to ourselves, families, churches, nation, and eternities will be beyond measure (2 Tim. 2:19, Deut. 28:1-13).

This is not starting something new. It is returning to something very old – a few critical Old Testament scriptures and some very critical original "good news" gospel scriptural principles that were taught by Jesus, Peter, Paul, John, James and others, to the early disciples and to the "early church". These speakers and writers were trying their very best to motivate followers to become "servants of righteousness" and "new creations".

## Hebrews 10:25-31

> Not forsaking the assembling of ourselves together, as the manner of some is; but exhorting one another: and so much the more, as ye see the day approaching. [26] For if we sin wilfully after that we have received the knowledge of the truth, there remaineth no more sacrifice for sins, [27] But a certain fearful

> looking for of judgment and fiery indignation, which shall devour the adversaries. [28] He that despised Moses' law died without mercy under two or three witnesses: [29] Of how much sorer punishment, suppose ye, shall he be thought worthy, who hath trodden under foot the Son of God, and hath counted the blood of the covenant, wherewith he was sanctified, an unholy thing, and hath done despite unto the Spirit of grace? [30] For we know him that hath said, Vengeance belongeth unto me, I will recompense, saith the Lord. And again, The Lord shall judge his people. [31] It is a fearful thing to fall into the hands of the living God.

Paul is not writing here to the general population. Scriptures prior to this passage reveal that he is writing to those in the church (vs. 25), some of whom are saved and possibly some who are not. This is not about a true Christian losing his salvation. This is addressed to a person who thinks he is saved but never became a true follower of Christ in the first place. After we have been saved by grace, we are not to carelessly, habitually, deliberately, or delightfully continue indulging in our sins. If we are truly saved in a relationship with Christ, we become "new creatures," using the power of Christ and His righteousness indwelling us and communicating with us to crucify the flesh and not let sin have dominion over us. <u>If we willfully continue to be servants of our sin nature, virtually mocking (trodding under foot) the precious Saviour and His Word, His name, His grace, His covenant, and His sacrifice, there are serious questions about our relationship with Him and therefore our salvation.</u> **Willful, consistent disobedience and evil doing are not compatible with the transformation power of a relationship with Jesus Christ!** This is precursory to our being probable recipients of Christ's "I never knew you" appraisal. <u>It doesn't get any more fearful that that.</u>

Please return and reread the second whole paragraph on page 2! Then please come back to here.

# WHAT ABOUT YOU (AND YOUR LOVED ONES)?

## 2 Cor. 13:5

> <u>Examine yourselves, whether ye be in the faith</u>; prove your own selves. Know ye not your own selves, how that <u>Jesus Christ is in you</u>...?

You can examine yourself in the genuineness of your salvation experience by prayerfully asking the Lord to help you know that when you told Him you believed in Him and called on Him to come into your heart and save you, you really "opened the door" to your heart and soul (mind, will, and emotions) and let the Lord's Spirit in (Rev. 3:15, 16, 20-22). When He is genuinely, wholeheartedly welcomed in, not just as your casual savior from hell but also as your active Lord, king, master, or controller (on earth and in heaven), He will affect your life in a host of very positive righteous wonderful, beneficial and powerful ways, some of which are mentioned below. (Romans 8:5-14)

If you have not let His Spirit in, or you have not grown to love the Lord, His Word and His ways and other people, the exercise below could be uncomfortable. The "good news" in this is that it is very fixable and the Lord would love to help you remedy this. Try to look up, think and pray regarding the scriptures.

Salvation is not a matter of adding up righteous acts vs. sins or just saying something with your physical mind and vocal cords. It is a matter of the **heart** and soul. Do you <u>really belong</u> to the Lord? (2 Tim. 2:19 **"NEVERTHELESS THE FOUNDATION OF GOD STANDETH SURE, HAVING THIS SEAL, THE LORD KNOWETH THEM THAT ARE HIS."**) Is His Spirit really joined with yours and is the Holy Spirit the major force and source in your life?

## Romans 8:9

> ... so be that the Spirit of God dwell in you. Now if any man <u>have not the Spirit of Christ,</u> HE IS NONE OF HIS.

Do you really believe in the blood sacrifice, death, burial and resurrection of Jesus as the Son of God? Does His life example and His relationship with you affect what you have become? **Does**

**He "know" you intimately as loving Him intensely and others whom He loves** (Matt. 7:23, 22:36—39, John 14:21)? Do you do what He says in His Word and from hearing His voice (or detecting His promptings) and obey these messages (John 10:26-28, Luke 6:46-47, Hebrews 12:24, 25)?

In the end times, do you feel the Lord will be able to say, "Welcome to My heaven, you good and faithful follower."? It is very scripturally plausible (Rev. 2 & 3) that He might discuss your faith and relationship (or lack thereof) with Him something along these lines – "I am very impressed (or disappointed) regarding:

1. Your faith and belief in Me and the way these have affected your life and relationship with Me (John 3:16-21, Rev. 2& 3).

2. The way you love Me intensely and others (#1 and #2 commandments in importance) and this had a profound effect on the way you responded to Me and My words and the way you loved and treated others (Rev. 2:4-7, John 14:21, Matt. 25:31-46, 1 John 3:10, John 10:26-28, Matt. 7:12, Prov. 8:17).

3. The way you genuinely asked Me and <u>let Me and My ways come into your life</u> as your Lord, Master or supreme authority (Rev. 3:20, John 14:23-24, 15:4-6, Romans 8:9).

4. The way you were able to repent and overcome iniquities and sins in your life (Luke 13:3, Rev. 2 & 3, note the rewards for repenting and overcoming). It is very obvious that in Rev. 2 & 3 the Lord is talking to individuals in churches. The "works" in these scriptures are not "working your way into heaven" works. They are the responses in your life showing who or what controls your life. They can be righteous or unrighteous.

5. The way I could describe you as spiritually "hot" being "good soil" and sought to do MY WILL by hearing, reading, learning, and <u>doing</u> My teachings and <u>praying frequently with Me</u> (Rev. 3:16, Matt. 13:18-23, Matt. 7:21-24, Luke 6:46-47, 1 Thess 5:11-23).

6. Your treatment of your mate I gave you. You did not treat your mate **treacherously** (over-delighting in others, not "forsaking all others", emotional snares with others, neglecting your mate or abusing them physically or emotionally, destroying your relationship with them (Mal.2:13-17).

7. Your ability to win and keep the hearts of your children so that you could spiritually guide them in My ways (Mal. 4:6, 2:15, Luke 1:16,17, Deut. 6:6,7).

8. Your ability to not be overcome with the world (1 John 5:4-5).

9. Your dedication and commitment to seeking first My kingdom in yourself and serving and helping others do likewise. (Matt. 20:26-28, Prov. 11:30)

10. The way you have kept your life in humbleness, holiness and purity (Prov. 16:18-19, 1 John 2:16-17, John 1:27, Matt. 5:1-16).

11. The way you spoke the truth and conducted your business or livelihood (Matt. 5:37, Amos 8:2, 4-7, 10-13).

12. From your intimate abiding relationship with Me – I was impressed with the way you were able to control your anger, forgive others, resist temptations, conquer bitterness, lust and other ungodly qualities (Matt. 6:15, 2 Tim. 3:1-7).

13. The way you never let your righteous works cause you to neglect your intimate relationship and communication with Me."

The above can serve as indicators or give you a general impression as to where you might stand spiritually being a "hot", "lukewarm", or "cold" "Believer". It can also show whether the Lord knows you as a true follower or as being without Him, neglecting His will, being selfish and overindulgent in sins and iniquities and overcome with the world.

Don Z. Weldon

## Rev. 3:15-16

I know thy works, that thou art neither cold nor hot: I would thou wert cold or hot. [16] So then because thou art lukewarm, and neither cold nor hot, I will spue thee out of my mouth.

Please do not mistakenly reason from the above that the Lord is more pleased with spiritually "cold" churches and individuals than lukewarm churches and individuals. Note how He feels about those in the "cold" church in Sardis (Rev. 3:1-6. Note the reward for overcoming.)

## Rev. 3:19-22 (solution to the above)

As many as I love, I rebuke and chasten: be zealous therefore, and **repent.** [20] Behold, I stand at the door, and knock: **if any man hear my voice, and open the door, I will come in to him,** and will sup with him, and he with me. [21] **To him that overcometh will I grant to sit with me in my throne, even as I also overcame, and am set down with my Father in his throne.** [22] He that hath an ear, let him hear what the Spirit saith unto the churches.

## Matthew 7:21

Not every one that saith unto me, Lord, Lord, shall enter into the kingdom of heaven; **but he that doeth the will of my Father** which is in heaven.

## Matthew 7:23

And then will I profess unto them, **I never knew you: depart from me, ye that work iniquity.**

## Matthew 7:24

**Therefore whosoever heareth these sayings of mine, and doeth them,** I will liken him unto a wise man, which built his house upon a rock:

Don't overly grieve if you or your loved ones did not and do not fare well in the above feeling you or they haven't become or done a lot of these things and would not be able to do so. You are right;

you or they can't do them! These are holy qualities and activities that come from the Lord. Your love of Him and the Holy Spirit's presence in your life will inspire and empower you to become and do them (John 15:5, 14:14-23, 1 John 5:1-5).

Possibly the greatest difficulty and hindrance for you to accept this can be that many beloved "passed on" friends, relatives, spiritual leaders' theologies and relationships with the Lord were not in line with these Lordship scriptures.

It is extremely hard to do but we must move on and help ourselves and those who are alive to have a chance to adopt and live these scriptures as part of our relationship with the Lord. Also, it is perfectly permissible scripturally for you to pray to the Lord that you and your loved ones love and obey the Lord more and more!

If you honestly feel deep in your soul that you love the Lord, His Word and ways and others, and have let His ways affect your life according to His will, and have a definite relationship with Him, you are in a great position for eternity with the Lord. If not, perhaps your best interest in heaven could be served by you thoroughly reviewing your relationship with the Lord and the impact this relationship has had or not had on what you have become and what you think, say and do. Our Lord is a powerful, magnificent, merciful, "commanding", holy, judging, wonderful God. He is very willing to help you become the "new creation" you are to be as His true follower. He desires that all become saved and requires that all His followers sin a lot less toward Him and others!

All this might sound overly complicated and overwhelming but the main emphasis boils down to this: Perhaps you need to ask the Lord to help you <u>genuinely</u> wholeheartedly <u>open the door</u> and <u>let Him and His ways</u> come into your heart and soul. Ask Him to forgive you for not doing this earlier and for all the subsequent sins. Tell Him that you purpose to love Him intensely, learn and obey His Words, let Him become your Lord and Master, and let Him help you repent and overcome things in your life hurting you and others around you and that are displeasing to Him. It will be possible to do His will if His Spirit is abiding in you and helping you with <u>His power</u> and the <u>power of your love of Him</u> helping you.

This concludes the synopsis (summary) of this book. If you are not yet fully convinced that to be saved you must become a "new creation" (becoming a genuine true follower of Jesus Christ in thinking, attitudes, and living in compliance to the Lordship scriptures), your best interest in Heaven could best be served by reading on.

**If at this point you are fully convinced that you want to become a Lordship Christian, then you probably should reread the synopsis and especially study the "What About You and Your Loved Ones?" section. It is most advisable that you look up each scripture in <u>your</u> Bible.**

> **\* It would be critical for you to look ahead and review pages 75-76 – "Easy Believism" Christianity and pages 76-77 – "Lordship Christianity".**

> **\* Also, the Bell Curve Righteousness Distribution discussion and diagram on pages 91-98 will help you determine if you are spiritually cold, lukewarm or hot!**

**Restate or re-pray your profession of faith to become a Lordship Christian and then discuss it with your pastor. He most likely would love to see you and many other church members become dedicated spiritually hot "new creations"!**

**If you are reading on, these next two sections done in 2005 and 2006 contain some additional powerful revelations, scriptures and principles. There will be much repetition, overlap and seemingly "overkill" but please bear with us. Our intentions are noble and God-directed. We want to insure as much as possible that there will be "no believer left behind". Major or even minor shifts in personal and congregational theology can be very slow and difficult. Easy believism scriptures and principles most likely have been repeated over and over to you for most of your**

**life. We pray that you will tolerate our repetition in the rest of this book and you will be eternally blessed!**

© 2007 No Believer Left Behind

# PREFACE TO *NO BELIEVER LEFT BEHIND* - **2005**

In Romans 1:21-22 scripture says that if we just "know" God but do not glorify Him (stir up, arouse or awaken ourselves – original language) as God (THE <u>SOVEREIGN</u> GOD OF EVERYTHING AND EVERYONE INCLUDING US), we will become weak and foolish in our thinking, decisions and actions. (See Titus 1:16) This can happen to churches, communities, and nations.

A careful prayerful review of the following statements from the writings of America's founding fathers and some subsequent presidents will reveal that America has foolishly spiritually and morally waned and wandered into some very big trouble! Our very future is at stake as to what we do about this trouble.

> "Of all the dispositions and habits which lead to political prosperity, religion and morality are indispensable supports. In vain would that man claim tribute to patriotism who should labor to subvert these great pillars of human happiness - these firmest props of the duties of men and citizens…reason and experience both forbid us to expect that national morality can prevail in exclusion of religious principles."
>
> George Washington

"God who gave us life gave us liberty. Can the liberties of a nation be secure when we have removed the conviction that these liberties are the gift of God? Indeed I tremble for my country when I reflect that God is just, that His justice cannot sleep forever."

Thomas Jefferson

"It is religion and morality alone which can establish the principles upon which freedom can securely stand. The only foundation of a free constitution is pure virtue, and if this cannot be inspired into our People in the greater measure than they have it now, they may change their Rulers and the forms of the Government, but they will not obtain a lasting liberty."

John Adams

"…The longer I live the more convincing proofs I see of this truth, that God governs in the affairs of men. And if a sparrow cannot fall to the ground without His notice, is it probable that an empire can rise without his aid? We have been assured, Sir, in the Sacred Writings that 'except the Lord build the house, they labor in vain that build it.'"

Benjamin Franklin

"And whereas it is the duty of nations as well as of men, to own their dependence upon the overruling power of God, to confess their sins and transgressions in humble sorrow, yet with assured hope that genuine repentance will lead to mercy and pardon; and to recognize the sublime truth announced in the Holy Scriptures and proven by all history, that those nations only are blessed whose God is the Lord."

Abraham Lincoln

"Let us look forward to the time when we can take the flag of our country and nail it below the Cross, and there let it wave as it waved in the olden times, and let us gather around it and inscribe for our motto: 'Liberty and union, one and inseparable, now and forever' and exclaim, 'Christ first, our country next!'"

Andrew Johnson

"We cannot read the history of our rising and development as a nation without reckoning with the place the Bible has occupied in shaping the advances of the Republic.   Where we have been the truest and most consistent in obeying its precepts, we have attained the greatest measure of contentment and prosperity."

Franklin Roosevelt

"Without God there is no virtue because there's no prompting of the conscience. Without God we are mired in the material, that flat world that tells us only what the senses perceive. Without God there is a coarsening of the society. Without God democracy will not and cannot long endure.   If we ever forget that we are one nation under God, then we will be a nation gone under."

Ronald Reagan

Although there are some bright spots, our national spiritual condition in general has gone from "Christian Light" to "Christian lite". Our "salt" has lost so much of its savor that it is very weak and being trodden underfoot of man. (Matt 5:13-16). It is very sobering to consider the destruction God historically brought over and over in Bible times to individuals, cities, and nations that had departed from His holy ways as far as we have.

How did we get into this spiritual vexation? Through a slow moving evolution in the theologies of some individuals influencing organized religion, we have <u>gravitated toward</u> scriptures (and interpretations) that allow us Christians to remain the lords of our own lives after we become "saved" believers or "followers" of the Lord.

We have <u>gravitated away from scriptures</u> and theologies that require us to let the Lord (God the Father, God the Son, and God the Holy Spirit) become our sovereign Lord and Master as we are going through the initial salvation experience and lifetime discipling processes.

For one small example, let's compare today's predominate theology with Abraham Lincoln's statements above. Genuine repentance (turning from sin, forsaking it and overcoming it) has fallen out of favor with most of today's doctrines on the matter. Agreeing with God that we have sinned, feeling sorry for our sins, and maybe confessing our sins (and slack or freedom to repeat them for the rest of our lives) has replaced genuine repentance.

It is very obvious that Lincoln ended this statement with the need for a significant (perhaps predominate) number of the citizens and leaders to GLORIFY HIM AS GOD.

Today many of us just think of our God as an "on call" need provider now and far into the future as our savior from an awful eternity. A personal relationship with our Lord and conducting our lives in compliance to His commands and teachings has become optional after becoming saved. Spiritual condition surveys and opinions by many in the ministry reveal that the minority of those professing belief and faith in Jesus Christ make Him their sovereign Lord and Master. The majority does not. The results have been disastrous!

All of this is supported by scripture. You will be amazed as you see the extent of the exclusion or neglect of highly critical scriptures that must be put into the creation of a Christian and put back into the development of a Christian. Our national church problems and circumstances support this. The struggles, defeats and victories of spiritually "cold, lukewarm and hot" Christians support this. The condition of our families and extent of food, drug and alcohol abuse supports this. Our governing problems support this.

This need for a major spiritual awakening and national call to genuine repentance is not a new modern man imagination and creativity project. It is the result of a very extensive long term non-denominational investigation involving dusting off and resurrecting very old scriptures that have been buried, forgotten, neglected or misinterpreted for years.

If you are in a spiritual leadership position, please pray as you go through this that you can reasonably distance yourself from the almost irresistible temptation to defend the current doctrinal systems of thought on these matters.  Please pray to avoid thinking that it is too uncomfortable to consider other things "outside the box" of what spiritually worked for you and other peers and leaders who trained or influenced you.  You likely were able to work out your salvation into an acceptable condition of spiritual excellence and the resultant victories.

However, speaking for the spiritually average Joes and Janes, "Most of us are having a very tough time doing what you did.  Our weaknesses, the world, flesh and the devil are really highly effective at destroying our ability to become and do what you are trying to teach us.  We've attended hundreds or thousands of religious meetings but still our families are in terrible trouble.  We're dysfunctional and/or breaking just as fast as the secular population.  Ninety percent of us admit on a survey that we have no personal relationship with Jesus Christ, and our children are vexing their souls into secular humanism and embracing all sorts of godlessness.  Many of us have very little evidence of periodic or sustained fruit of the Spirit (Gal. 5:22-24) – love, joy, peace, kindness, goodness, faithfulness, gentleness and self control).  According to many authorities on the matter, many of us think we are saved but we're really not.  Please help us!  Probably our earthly and eternal destinies depend on you to help us in our plight."

With massive inclusion of these powerful scriptures into the evangelism process and developing a Christian, <u>there is great hope</u>!

# NO BELIEVER LEFT BEHIND - 2005

## ETERNITY – A LONG, LONG TIME

Where a person spends eternity after a short life on earth is the most important of all issues in every person's life - whether in heaven, hell, or as some think, scattered as billions of meaningless atoms in food chains, water, atmosphere or dirt with the person's conscious being completely disappearing forever as a wisp of smoke!

Many individuals and religious organizations that exist to create a means for a person to attain their eternal destiny in heaven must become aware of many Satan inspired man-made errors that have crept into evangelism and discipleship. These have gradually evolved through many years and no particular person or generation is totally at fault.

There is currently a growing ground-swell awareness that possibly fifty plus percent of those professing to be Christians today and fully expecting to go to heaven are not "saved" at all! One very well known authority in the subject of salvation is reported to have said that he doubts if even fifteen percent are saved. Another says that church members "professed" to be saved are possibly the "ripest fields unto harvest" to become "genuinely" saved.

It is incredible that so little ministry is focused on helping these unsaved "Christians" become aware of their condition and unexpected destiny and how to change their destiny! Since they have followed the procedures to become saved as possibly directed by their leaders, most unsaved believers do not know who they are nor are they worried about it.

This notion is not the brain-child of human reasoning. It comes from increasing observable evidence regarding the extent of flagrant unabated shameful attitudes and misbehavior of "christians" and their tragic destructions on evangelism and the health and well being of families and our nation. Let's minimize the endless winless war on the <u>symptoms</u> (flagrant unrighteousness) of this problem and swallow some doctrinal pride and maximize going after the <u>cause</u> (believers who do not really become saved and continue violating God's ways after making a profession of faith) of the problem. Victory in this will lead to solving many individual, family, church, business, cultural and political problems!

This notion is also a new awareness that comes from reinstalling a multitude of holy scriptures that have fallen into neglect and misinterpretation and putting them back into the process of <u>creating a Christian</u> (evangelism) and <u>developing a Christian</u> (discipleship). We promise you will be amazed as we go through this. Whether or not you are in the "saved" or "unsaved" groups, everyone must become aware and come to grips with these scriptures.

Let's explore this whole idea asking God to reveal His truth! Please postpone defending your current theology on these matters until you see the whole picture. Prayerfully let the Holy Scriptures be your major focus.

Here are the very basic "gold standard" (widely accepted and used) scriptures in becoming a Christian:

## John 3:16

> For God so loved the world, that he gave his only begotten Son, that whosoever believeth in him should not perish, but have everlasting life.

## Ephes. 2:8-9

> For by grace are ye saved through faith; and that not of yourselves: it is the gift of God: [9] Not of works, lest any man should boast.

## Romans 10:9

> That if thou shalt confess with thy mouth the Lord Jesus, and shalt believe in thine heart that God hath raised him from the dead, thou shalt be saved.

## 2 Cor. 5:21

> For he hath made him to be sin for us, who knew no sin; that we might be made the righteousness of God in him.

## Romans 10:13

> For whosoever shall call upon the name of the Lord shall be saved.

## 1 John 1:9

> If we confess our sins, he is faithful and just to forgive us our sins, and to cleanse us from all unrighteousness.

There is no shortcoming or problem with these wonderful scriptures. They have been used for centuries to "save" millions.

The shortcomings and problems lie with what some individuals and denominations have done with the gold standard salvation scriptures. For many, they become their whole theology and do not embrace or pay any attention to what else the Bible says about salvation.

# NEGLECTED SALVATION SCRIPTURES

Why do we put so much <u>eternity stock</u> in these scriptures when there are so many other scriptures that are highly critical and relevant to a person's salvation?

We will answer this question after we explore <u>some</u> of the other scriptures that are screaming for attention to get into evangelism and discipleship. Please carefully read these two or more times now as they are EXTREMELY important and will be referred to frequently.

## Matthew 7:21

Not every one that saith unto me, Lord, Lord, shall enter into the kingdom of heaven; but he that doeth the will of my Father which is in heaven.

## Luke 13:23-24

Then said one unto him, Lord, are there few that be saved? And he said unto them,

[24] Strive to enter in at the strait gate: for many, I say unto you, will seek to enter in, and shall not be able.

## Luke 13:28

There shall be weeping and gnashing of teeth, when ye shall see Abraham, and Isaac, and Jacob, and all the prophets, in the kingdom of God, and you yourselves thrust out.

## Luke 6:46

And why call ye me, Lord, Lord, and do not the things which I say?

## Luke 13:3

I tell you, Nay: but, except ye repent, ye shall all likewise perish.

## Matthew 22:36-39

Master, which is the great commandment in the law? [37] Jesus said unto him, Thou shalt love the Lord thy God with all thy heart, and with all thy soul, and with all thy mind. [38] This is the first and great commandment. [39] And the second is like unto it, Thou shalt love thy neighbour as thyself.

## John 14:21

He that hath my commandments, and keepeth them, he it is that loveth me....

## John 14:23

Jesus answered and said unto him, If a man love me, he will keep my words: and my Father will love him, and we will come unto him, and make our abode with him.

## 1 John 4:15

Whosoever shall confess that Jesus is the Son of God, God dwelleth in him, and he in God.

## Romans 8:9

But ye are not in the flesh, but in the Spirit, if so be that the Spirit of God dwell in you. Now if any man have not the Spirit of Christ, he is none of his.

## 1 John 2:6

He that saith he abideth in him ought himself also so to walk, even as he walked.

"Ought" in the original language of this verse means a genuine indwelt Christian "must, is under obligation, or bound and indebted" to live according to Christ's example and instructions,

## Romans 10:2-3

For I bear them record that they have a zeal of God, but not according to knowledge. [3] For they being ignorant of God's righteousness, and going about to establish their own righteousness, have not submitted themselves unto the righteousness of God.

## Ephes. 2:8-10

For by grace are ye saved through faith; and that not of yourselves: it is the gift of God: [9] Not of works, lest any man should boast. [10] For we are his workmanship, created in Christ Jesus unto good works, which God hath before ordained that we should walk in them. (Verse 10 is often missing from the gold standard scripture passages.)

## Matthew 28:19-20

Go ye therefore, and teach all nations, baptizing them in the name of the Father, and of the Son, and of the Holy Ghost: [20] Teaching them to <u>observe all things</u> whatsoever I have commanded you: and, lo, I am with you alway, even unto the end of the world. Amen.

## James 2:17

Even so faith, if it hath not works, is dead, being alone.

## Galatians 5:24

And they that are Christ's have crucified the flesh with the affections and lusts.

## Romans 6:18

Being then made free from sin, ye became the servants of righteousness.

## Romans 8:1-2

There is therefore now no condemnation to them which are in Christ Jesus, who walk not after the flesh, but after the Spirit. [2] For the law of the Spirit of life in Christ Jesus hath made me free from the law of sin and death.

## 1 John 2:4

He that saith, I know him, and keepeth not his commandments, is a liar, and the truth is not in him.

## 2 Cor. 5:17

Therefore if any man be in Christ, he is a new creature: old things are passed away; behold, all things are become new.

These scriptures are not printed in the Bible with dimmer ink or smaller letters than were the gold standard scriptures. They have just as much right to be included in the salvation process as any other scripture relevant to the leading of people to the Lord and discipling them. They cannot be denied and must not be overlooked.

Apparently, for many "new and old converts, it is very difficult for them to accept and practice these challenging scriptures and principles during the discipleship process (or the rest of their lives) if during the evangelism process they are told and persuaded that all they have to do to be saved and go to heaven is focus their conversion around the gold standard scriptures. Much of the conversion process today could be compared to getting a person to sign a contract agreeing to a matter and then shortly thereafter (or through years of sermons) presenting them with many pages of unexpected small print additional requirements that go along with the signed contract.

Many reject this notion and react with apathy toward any attempt to help them grow spiritually or in obedience to the Lord since they want to and in fact feel that the main issue, going to heaven and avoiding hell, is taken care of with the simple gold standard statements or prayers and commitments.

Please avoid the temptation as you go through this book to think that it is theology based upon "salvation by works." It is NOT! It is however a very strong scriptural affirmation that if a person is a genuine, new birth, and saved follower of our Lord, he will have much success at righteous living. He will seek first the kingdom of God and think and act like he belongs in it.

## WHAT'S THE PROBLEM?

Let's answer now the question about why we put so much eternity stock in the gold standard scriptures and neglect the additional scriptures "screaming for attention".

First of all, the gold standard scriptures can and do save a person. Many who profess a desire to become a Christian based on these scriptures develop a personal abiding or indwelling relationship with the Lord, read and love His Word, live their lives following the Lord and are saved. In principle, these can be described and understood in the "parable of the sower" (next page) as those whose soul is "good ground" - upon hearing the words of the kingdom, they go further with the Lord than just "believing" and "calling on the Lord to be saved".

There are many, however, who only want to recognize and live the gold standard scriptures because these scriptures, (which basically have no righteousness requirements,) taken alone without the "neglected" scriptures (and other scripture) allow these people "in their own eyes" to create their own personal custom salvation and discipling plans and their own lifestyle. This allows them to basically become and do whatever they want after becoming a "Christian". They have no interest or intention in a personal relationship with Jesus and allowing Him to be their Lord <u>and Master</u>, becoming and doing what He says. Tragically, they conclude that righteous living and having an effective life changing relationship with the Lord have nothing to do with their salvation.

## Deut. 12:8

> Ye shall not do after all the things that we do here this day, every man whatsoever is right in his own eyes.

Evidently, through the years, individuals and churches have promoted the gold standard scriptures in personal evangelism and altar calls because they are simple, fit into pocket tracts, are fast to convey, and since they typically require little or no righteousness commitments, the likelihood increases that the person being evangelized will "accept Christ as their Savior". What happens after that will be discussed later.

Whenever a government creates a new law, immediately those who want to circumvent the law look for <u>loopholes</u> so that they can still do most or all they did before the new law. Many who make professions of faith do this and can be understood and described in principle as those with souls like "wayside" (hard packed), "stony or thorny" soil. Deep within their minds, wills and emotions they are only desiring to avoid hell, hopefully go to heaven, with no intention of letting the Lord really come into their life, truly following Jesus, or becoming "a new creation" – what some call "easy believism". The gold standard scriptures, they feel, allow them to freely exercise loopholes!

The rest of the Bible and especially the neglected, overlooked or misinterpreted scriptures when recognized and understood close the loopholes and reeks havoc on easy believism!

*No Believer Left Behind*

God's Word is powerful, communicating with Him is powerful, His abiding in us is powerful, His grace is powerful. A love relationship with Him and His Word can change hard wayside dirt, stony soil and thorny soil into "good ground"! We must preach and teach the neglected and misinterpreted scriptures frequently. Since these scriptures are in the Bible, Spirit-filled Christ-indwelt leaders will do this even though their followers might not appreciate it at first.

The souls of many "lost Christians" can become "good ground" as they discover their errors and become properly motivated to establish a personal effective relationship with the Lord and live His righteousness. We will discuss "motivation" later.

## PARABLE OF THE SOWER

### Matthew 13:3-8

And he spake many things unto them in parables, saying, Behold, a sower went forth to sow; [4] And when he sowed, some seeds fell by the <u>way side</u>, and the fowls came and devoured them up: [5] Some fell upon <u>stony places</u>, where they had not much earth: and forthwith they sprung up, because they had no deepness of earth: [6] And when the sun was up, they were scorched; and because they had no root, they withered away. [7] And some fell among <u>thorns</u>; and the thorns sprung up, and choked them: [8] But other fell into good ground, and brought forth fruit, some an hundredfold, some sixtyfold, some thirtyfold.

### Matthew 13:18-23   (Jesus' explanation of the parable)

Hear ye therefore the parable of the sower. [19] When any one heareth the <u>word of the kingdom</u>, and understandeth it not, then cometh the wicked one, and catcheth away that which was sown in his heart. This is he which received seed by the <u>way side</u>. [20] But he that received the seed into <u>stony places</u>, the same is he that heareth the word, and anon with joy receiveth it; [21] Yet hath he not root in himself, but dureth for a while: for when tribulation or persecution ariseth because of the word, by and by he is offended. [22] He also that received seed among the

<u>thorns</u> is he that heareth the word; and the care of this world, and the deceitfulness of riches, choke the word, and he becometh unfruitful. [23] But he that received seed into the <u>good ground</u> is he that heareth the word, and understandeth it; which also beareth fruit, and bringeth forth, some an hundredfold, some sixty, some thirty.

Upon hearing and saying the <u>words of the kingdom</u> regarding salvation, many in the churches quickly and easily have the words snatched way by Satan, or soon become apathetic to or reject the words, or the word is nullified by the pressures and pursuits of life. They went into the salvation process with selfish souls that were unprepared, improperly informed, unteachable, unmotivated, and over-indulgent in the world. They came out the same way – with no personal Lord and no salvation.

It is painfully interesting to consider that it is possible the four soils can be thought of in terms of a "bell curve normal distribution". The hard packed, stony and thorny soils, or souls should we say, when presented with the words of the Lord, react "cold or lukewarm" representing the large majority of the population hearing the words, the "spiritually hot" group being the remaining small minority.

If there is any degree of truth to this, is it any wonder why our spiritual leaders have such difficulties motivating us in their sermons and lessons to obedience to God's Word and to serve in His kingdom? As mentioned earlier, this can change with unwavering preaching and teaching the powerful neglected and misinterpreted scriptures.

## OUR LORD'S REQUIREMENTS

Threaded throughout the Bible is a major theme of righteousness that cannot be denied. Our Lord comprised of God the Father, God the Son and God the Holy Spirit fully intends for those who are His followers, though not perfect, to be very successful in being holy, moral, righteous, good, loving and obedient to <u>His</u> ways. The coming of Jesus Christ, His blood sacrifice, and His grace did not change this as we will see.

## Jeremiah 18:7-8

At what instant I shall speak concerning a nation, and concerning a kingdom, to pluck up, and to pull down, and to destroy it; [8] If that nation, against whom I have pronounced, turn from their evil, I will repent of the evil that I thought to do unto them.

## Jeremiah 18:11-12

Now therefore go to, speak to the men of Judah, and to the inhabitants of Jerusalem, saying, Thus saith the Lord; Behold, I frame evil against you, and devise a device against you: return ye now every one from his evil way, <u>and make your ways and your doings good.</u> [12] And they said, THERE IS NO HOPE: but we will walk after our own devices, and we will every one do the imagination of his evil heart.

## Jeremiah 18:17

I will scatter them as with an east wind before the enemy; I will shew them the back, and not the face, in the day of their calamity.

## 2 Peter 3:9

The Lord is not slack concerning his promise, as some men count slackness; but is longsuffering to us-ward, not willing that any should perish, but that all should come to repentance.

## 1 Peter 1:15-16

But as he which hath called you is holy, so be ye holy in all manner of conversation; [16] Because it is written, Be ye holy; for I am holy.

## Matthew 13:41-43

The Son of man shall send forth his angels, and they shall gather out of his kingdom all things that offend, and them which do iniquity; [42] And shall cast them into a furnace of fire: there shall be wailing and gnashing of teeth. [43] Then shall the righteous shine forth as the sun in the kingdom of their Father. Who hath ears to hear, let him hear.

## Numbers 15:40

That ye may remember, and do all my commandments, and be holy unto your God.

## 1 Thes. 4:7

For God hath not called us unto uncleanness, but unto holiness.

Jesus says:

## Luke 13:3

I tell you, Nay: but, except ye repent, ye shall all likewise perish.

God sent His Son, Jesus, to provide us with the power and ability to meet His holy requirements in His Word. He didn't send Jesus so that we could just "believe" or have faith that He is who He says He is and thereby attain eternal life with Him – EASY BELIEVISM. He came so that those believers who choose, can and will unequivocally invite and admit Him into our heart and soul, make Him our Lord, Master, and sovereign authority, letting His presence, Word and power in us be the main driving forces in our lives – LORDSHIP. Believing is the first non-optional critical step to begin this process.

When He comes into our heart and soul, He brings many righteous changes into our lives including beginning the process of getting rid of sin tendencies and inspiring us in doing many righteous deeds (unfortunately many "easy believism" proponents call these "works" which has a negative connotation related to salvation by leaving off verse 10 of Ephesians 2:8-10).

There are several scriptural passages that those immersed in easy believism will embrace, thinking the passages are loopholes to justify unrighteous living after becoming saved. Unfortunately for them, many times another set of scriptures very close by blow the loopholes away (as in the Ephes. 2:8-10 passages).

For instance, I Cor. 3:13-15 gives the impression that a righteous man and an unrighteous man's activities will not matter when it comes to being saved. Easy believism rests heavily upon these scriptures.

## 1 Cor. 3:13-15

> Every man's work shall be made manifest: for the day shall declare it, because it shall be revealed by fire; and the fire shall try every man's work of what sort it is. [14] If any man's work abide which he hath built thereupon, he shall receive a reward. [15] If any man's work shall be burned, he shall suffer loss: but he himself shall be saved; yet so as by fire.

The very next two scriptures greatly undermine any comfort in flirtation with the above interpretation because they reveal a malignancy. If we are a true follower of the Lord, He dwells in us as His temple and He is <u>very</u> concerned that His temple is kept holy! When you consider the other neglected Lordship scriptures, this easy believism crutch is completely broken.

## 1 Cor. 3:16-17

> Know ye not that ye are the temple of God, and that the Spirit of God dwelleth in you? [17] If any man defile the temple of God, him shall God destroy; for the temple of God is holy, which temple ye are.

In very young converts who have little or no major evil to repent from, the Lord converts them from the major evil tendencies and unrighteousness that would later come to them had they no relationship with Him.

## WHO SAYS RIGHTEOUSNESS AND LORDSHIP HAVE ANYTHING TO DO WITH BEING SAVED?

Let's explore some of the highlights. Our Lord says in John 3:16-21 that if we truly believe in Him, we will attain eternal life. If we do not truly believe in Him, we will perish. If we <u>say or think we believe</u> but we are not truly attracted to Jesus, hate His truth and light, and continue to love and live in darkness, we "believeth not" in Jesus Christ and are condemned along with nonbelievers. He that truly believes and that is not condemned is attracted to Jesus' light, lives His truth such that his deeds or actions indicate that he and the Lord are "engaged together" in the way he lives his life! (look up "wrought" in the original Greek language as it pertains to John 3:21)

Jesus Christ and His ways cannot be separated, and if He is believed in, asked in, and is genuinely allowed to come into a person's heart and life, He brings His righteous ways with Him. This starts affecting the way the new Believer lives his life!

## John 3:16-21

> For God so loved the world, that he gave his only begotten Son, that whosoever believeth in him should not perish, but have everlasting life. [17] For God sent not his Son into the world to condemn the world; but that the world through him might be saved.
>
> [18] <u>He that believeth on him is not condemned</u>: <u>but he</u> that believeth not is condemned already, because he hath not believed in the name of the only begotten Son of God. [19] And this is the condemnation, that light is come into the world, and men loved darkness rather than light, because their deeds were evil. [20] For every one that doeth evil hateth the light, neither cometh to the light, lest his deeds should be reproved. [21] <u>But he that doeth truth cometh to the light, that his deeds may be made manifest, that they are wrought in God.</u>

A very careful reading will reveal that with the location of the two "but he's", the first phrase of verse 18 goes with verse 21!

Paul says in a <u>lengthy continuous discussion</u> in Romans chapters 4-8 that the "imputed" righteousness that comes through true faith and belief, not through works, is intended to result in the believer being free from the dominion of sins, able to crucify sins of the flesh and to become a servant of righteousness.

## Romans 4:3

> For what saith the scripture? Abraham believed God, and it was counted unto him for righteousness.

## Romans 4:6

Even as David also describeth the blessedness of the man, unto whom God imputeth righteousness without works,

## Romans 4:24

But for us also, to whom it shall be imputed, if we believe on him that raised up Jesus our Lord from the dead;

## Romans 6:1-2

What shall we say then? Shall we continue in sin, that grace may abound? [2] God forbid. How shall we, that are dead to sin, live any longer therein?

## Romans 6:6

Knowing this, that our old man is crucified with him, that the body of sin might be destroyed, that henceforth we should not serve sin.

## Romans 6:14

For sin shall not have dominion over you: for ye are not under the law, but under grace.

## Romans 6:18

Being then made free from sin, ye became the servants of righteousness.

## Romans 8:1-2

There is therefore now no condemnation to them which are in Christ Jesus, who walk not after the flesh, but after the Spirit. [2] For the law of the Spirit of life in Christ Jesus hath made me free from the law of sin and death.

## Romans 8:9-10

But ye are not in the flesh, but in the Spirit, if so be that the Spirit of God dwell in you. Now if any man have not the Spirit of Christ, HE IS NONE OF HIS. [10] And if Christ be in you, the body is dead because of sin; but the Spirit is life because of righteousness.

## Ephes. 2:8-10

For by grace are ye saved through faith; and that not of yourselves: it is the gift of God: [9] Not of works, lest any man should boast. [10] <u>For we are his workmanship, created in Christ Jesus unto good works, which God hath before ordained that we should walk in them.</u>

James says for us to live in obedience to God's Word and that faith involving belief without righteous actions is dead.

## James 1:22

But be ye doers of the word, and not hearers only, deceiving your own selves.

## James 2:14-17

What doth it profit, my brethren, though a man say he hath faith, and have not works? can faith save him? [15] If a brother or sister be naked, and destitute of daily food, [16] And one of you say unto them, Depart in peace, be ye warmed and filled; notwithstanding ye give them not those things which are needful to the body; what doth it profit? [17] Even so faith, if it hath not works, is dead, being alone.

Satan and his followers "believe", but they aren't saved.

## James 2:19

Thou believest that there is one God; thou doest well: the devils also believe, and tremble.

## James 4:17

Therefore to him that knoweth to do good, and doeth it not, to him it is sin.

## James 2:21-22

Was not Abraham our father justified by works, when he had offered Isaac his son upon the altar? [22] Seest thou how <u>faith wrought with his works, and by works was faith made perfect?</u>

Jesus indicates the importance of righteous living as it pertains to salvation.

## Matthew 13:41-43

The Son of man shall send forth his angels, and they shall gather out of his kingdom all things that offend, and them which do iniquity; [42] And shall cast them into a furnace of fire: there shall be wailing and gnashing of teeth. [43] Then shall the righteous shine forth as the sun in the kingdom of their Father. Who hath ears to hear, let him hear.

Peter makes a particularly strong assertion that we MUST add righteous qualities to our faith (and belief) in order to insure our eternal destiny with our Lord.

If we try to add and live these qualities through human effort, we will totally fail. They must come about from our Lord enabling us to do them from a powerful abiding relationship with Him.

## 2 Peter 1:4-11

Whereby are given unto us exceeding great and precious promises: that by these ye might be partakers of the divine nature, having escaped the corruption that is in the world through lust. [5] And beside this, giving all diligence, <u>add to your faith</u> virtue; and to virtue knowledge; [6] And to knowledge temperance; and to temperance patience; and to patience godliness; [7] And to godliness brotherly kindness; and to brotherly kindness charity. [8] For if these things be in you, and abound, they make you that ye shall neither be barren nor unfruitful in the knowledge of our Lord Jesus Christ. [9] But he that lacketh these things is blind, and cannot see afar off, and hath forgotten that <u>he was purged from his old sins.</u> [10] <u>Wherefore the rather, brethren, give diligence to make your calling and election sure: for if ye do</u>

> these things, ye shall never fall: [11] For so an entrance shall be ministered unto you abundantly into the everlasting kingdom of our Lord and Saviour Jesus Christ.

## John 15:5

> I am the vine, ye are the branches: He that abideth in me, and I in him, the same bringeth forth much fruit: for without me ye can do nothing.

All of these New Testament scriptures are dramatically parallel to what God told Moses about our intended proper relationship with Him (basically a Lordship relationship). God does not change. Obviously, we first have to have belief and faith in order to do these righteous things in these verses.

## Deut. 10:12-13

> And now, Israel, what doth the Lord thy God require of thee, but to fear the Lord thy God, to walk in all his ways, and to love him, and to serve the Lord thy God with all thy heart and with all thy soul, [13] To keep the commandments of the Lord, and his statutes, which I command thee this day for thy good?

Christ's coming and His grace did not erase God's requirements in the Ten Commandments or in a lot of the Old Testament. In the New Testament, He added to them and made some of them more challenging but all of them easier if we have a strong abiding relationship with Him. For example:

## Matthew 5:17-18

> Think not that I am come to destroy the law, or the prophets: I am not come to destroy, but to fulfil. [18] For verily I say unto you, Till heaven and earth pass, one jot or one tittle shall in no wise pass from the law, till all be fulfilled.

## Matthew 5:21-22

> Ye have heard that it was said by them of old time, Thou shalt not kill; and whosoever shall kill shall be in danger of the judgment: [22] But I say unto you, That whosoever is angry with his

brother without a cause shall be in danger of the judgment: and whosoever shall say to his brother, Raca, shall be in danger of the council: but whosoever shall say, Thou fool, shall be in danger of hell fire.

## Matthew 5:27-28

Ye have heard that it was said by them of old time, Thou shalt not commit adultery: [28] But I say unto you, That whosoever looketh on a woman to lust after her hath committed adultery with her already in his heart.

## Matthew 5:32

But I say unto you, That whosoever shall put away his wife, saving for the cause of fornication, causeth her to commit adultery: and whosoever shall marry her that is divorced committeth adultery.

## Matthew 5:44

But I say unto you, Love your enemies, bless them that curse you, do good to them that hate you, and pray for them which despitefully use you, and persecute you;

## 1 John 5:3-5

For this is the love of God, that we keep his commandments: and his commandments are not grievous. (*overly burdensome – original language*) [4] For whatsoever is born of God overcometh the world: and this is the victory that overcometh the world, even our faith. [5] Who is he that overcometh the world, but he that believeth that Jesus is the Son of God?

In 1 John we see more evidence that there are no loopholes giving us freedom to ignore becoming and doing what our Lord says after we become "saved".

## 1 John 1:5-10

This then is the message which we have heard of him, and declare unto you, that God is light, and in him is no darkness at all. [6] If we say that we have fellowship with him, and walk in darkness, we lie, and do not the truth: [7] But if we walk in the light, as

> he is in the light, we have fellowship one with another, and the blood of Jesus Christ his Son cleanseth us from all sin. [8] If we say that we have no sin, we deceive ourselves, and the truth is not in us. [9] If we confess our sins, he is faithful and just to forgive us our sins, and to cleanse us from all unrighteousness. [10] If we say that we have not sinned, we make him a liar, and his word is not in us.

Looking for and practicing loopholes, many in our day like to give allegiance in this passage only to verse 9 in their personal theology which they feel gives them freedom to continue living in darkness and to just confess their sins and then they are all cleaned up so they can continue to live in darkness until the next confession – a process that can go on for a lifetime. They never become motivated to crucify their sin nature or become a servant of righteousness. This is great error.

By reviewing the surrounding and nearby scriptures of verse 9, we get the true meaning. <u>Only those who have a close fellowship with Him, walking in the light as He is in the light, can receive and benefit from His atoning blood sacrifice and be cleansed from sin</u>. Obviously, a genuinely born-again convert receives this when he becomes saved.

Highly critical to being able to walk in the light as He is in the Light is a close indwelling Lordship relationship with Jesus. This relationship is thereby critical to our being able to do His will and keep His commandments.

## 1 John 2:1-6

> My little children, these things write I unto you, that ye sin not. And if any man sin, we have an advocate with the Father, Jesus Christ the righteous: [2] And he is the propitiation for our sins: and not for ours only, but also for the sins of the whole world. [3] <u>And hereby we do know that we know him, if we keep his commandments</u>. [4] He that saith, <u>I know him, and keepeth not his commandments, is a liar</u>, and the truth is not in him. [5] But whoso keepeth his word, in him verily is the love of God perfected: hereby know we that we are in him. [6] He that saith he abideth in him ought himself also so to walk, even as he walked.

## 1 John 2:17

> And the world passeth away, and the lust thereof: but he that doeth the will of God abideth for ever.

## Matthew 7:21

> Not every one that saith unto me, Lord, Lord, shall enter into the kingdom of heaven; but he that doeth the will of my Father which is in heaven.

## 1 John 2:29

> If ye know that he is righteous, ye know that every one that doeth righteousness is born of him.

If the confessing does not have any degree of repentance and overcoming (turning from the sin) involved and the person stays in complete bondage to the confessed sin, there is a strong possibility there is no indwelling relationship. Remaining under the dominion of sin is not compatible with the transformation power of a relationship with Jesus Christ! Those observing or involved will perceive this person's faith or belief as hypocritical or as a mockery and want nothing to do with Christianity.

The Hindu leader, Gandhi, when working out his faith was strongly attracted to and complimentary of Christianity but concluded, "I could become a Christian if it weren't for Christians!" He was literally grossed out by the massive shameful extent of unrighteous attitudes, sins and iniquities he observed in the Christians he came in contact with.

The basic intent of this book is to turn this situation around. In Christianity, we simply must not embrace a few salvation scriptures and ignore many others on the same subject that reveal the absolute necessity for Christ's followers to become holy, righteous and obedient to His Word and promptings!

Jesus sums up the issue when he in effect says that many are not able to call Him Lord because they do not do what He says!

## Luke 6:46

> And why call ye me, Lord, Lord, and do not the things which I say?

He also says that many who call Him Lord will be told to "depart from Him" because <u>they did not do God's will which is hearing and doing what He says</u>. God's will is not just related to choosing a wife, career, place to live and work, etc. It is how to think and act in compliance to His Word and promptings.

## Matthew 7:21-24

> Not every one that saith unto me, Lord, Lord, shall enter into the kingdom of heaven; <u>but he that doeth the will of my Father</u> which is in heaven. [22] Many will say to me in that day, Lord, Lord, have we not prophesied in thy name? and in thy name have cast out devils? and in thy name done many wonderful works? [23] And then will I profess unto them, I never knew you: depart from me, ye that work iniquity.
>
> [24 <u>**THEREFORE WHOSOEVER HEARETH**</u> these sayings of mine, and <u>**DOETH**</u> them, I will liken him unto a wise man, which built his house upon a rock:

Please do not look for a personal loophole and fall into the temptation that Matt. 7:21-24 applies only to "false prophets". Christ says the solution to being told "depart from Me" is in the phrase, "<u>therefore whosoever</u>" (anybody, everybody) that hears, (reads, learns) and does what He says is a very wise person.... Doing God's will is the heart of these scriptures. Anyone (including false prophets) not hearing and doing what He says is not doing His will! Also producing "evil fruit" can be done by anyone, not just false prophets (Matt 7:15-19).

How did we get in this awful situation with so many "Christians" living unbridled, spiritually and morally out of control?

We have discussed the "gold standard" problem, the neglected and misinterpreted scriptures problem, the loopholes problem and the selfish soils problems. However there are some other fundamental problems that contribute to this overall situation.

## DOING CONVERSION WRONG

During the conversion process (initial steps of becoming a Christian) the new "believer" can make some fatal mistakes. He can believe, have faith and "call on the Lord to be saved but believe and decide with his selfish will and darkness-loving heart that the Lord is or might be the Lord of the universe and others, but is not going to be <u>his</u> own personal Lord. Tragically, this can easily happen because he might be doing exactly what the one leading him to Christ says he has to do to be saved.

### Romans 1:21

> Because that, when they knew God, <u>they glorified him not as God, neither were thankful</u>; but became vain in their imaginations, and their foolish heart was darkened.

In two of the gold standard scriptures (Romans 10:9,13), if we confess and call on the Lord as if He is "the" Lord, or everybody else's Lord, but is not going to be "our" Lord, Master, and Supreme Authority, then we do our conversion wrong. This can be verified by referring to the definition of "Lord" in the original language in these scriptures.

As a consequence of this, the new "convert" can become an eternal victim of his foolish, selfish free will. At the point of salvation when he prays or commits "to receive Christ" he can actually refuse to let Christ abide in or indwell him. While saying the prayer for Christ to come into his life, his free will can decide to keep Him out. Our Lord will not override insincerity or selfish free will.

Soon after a multitude of "easy believism" sermons he can easily decide that he can still stay boss of his own life. He, by not allowing Jesus to indwell in him and become his Lord and Master, is predisposed and easily becomes a foolish victim to decide not to love the Lord and others, not to respond appropriately to God's grace, not to study God's Word or pray, not to live according to Christ's ways, but continue to live in darkness. This is doing his conversion <u>wrong</u>!

He can choose to be "lukewarm" about his faith and settle into "playing church", become a spiritual drop-out, going to church on Christmas and Easter (or every Sunday) or to increase in his sins and iniquities because he feels he is free to do so. Tragically, he can even slip into being the most foul spiritually degenerate person possible and feel he will still be admitted into heaven.

## NON-OPTIONAL REPENTANCE

Embodied in the failings that can take place during the conversion process is the <u>absence of an all important major component</u> of salvation that has fallen into major disfavor and neglect in modern theology. We must reintroduce "repentance" into the conversion and discipleship process! Repentance is the ability to "turn from" something bad (contrary to God's will), and "turn to" something good (in line with God's will).

Remember, we have seen that many are genuinely "born again" (establishing the Lord as Lord and Master) as they "do their salvation experience right. A crucial outcome as these new converts respond appropriately to power of the redeeming blood sacrifice of Jesus Christ's death and resurrection and grace is that <u>with Jesus' Spirit abiding in them they posses a repentant heart</u>, (the desire and ability to change - a teachable spirit).

How important is this ability to change? Jesus Christ says, "I tell you, Nay: but, except ye repent, ye shall all likewise perish." (Luke 13:3) "Repent" and "repentance" in this verse as defined in the original Greek is "through sorrow and guilt to reconsider and think differently leading to reversal and reformation." This means that with non-perishing salvation, we not only are to confess our sins, with Jesus indwelling us, we have the power to REPENT of our sins (turn from them and <u>overcome</u> them.)

It is very important to note and focus on some of our Lord's statements to the churches in Revelation 2 and 3 and some statements that He did not make. These church members were indulging in things that were very displeasing to the Lord that very uncomfortably parallel much "Christian" behavior today.

First, He <u>did not</u> say, "Because you say you believe in Me and called on Me to come into your life and to save you, therefore your departures from Me and My ways are all forgiven and forgotten and heaven is yours." He told them to <u>repent</u> of and <u>overcome</u> these things in no uncertain terms and in doing so there would be a GREAT REWARD! There is no insinuation here that a Lordship Christian would lose their salvation! (See chart – next page.)

Jesus did not tell the woman caught in adultery that she had His permission to continue in her lifestyle as long as she "believed" in Him and confessed that she had sinned. He told her in no uncertain terms to repent and overcome ("Go and sin no more.").

In Romans 7:14-24, we need to be careful not to misinterpret and misapply Paul's description of himself in his "old man" carnal state – totally under the captivity of the "law of sin" (vs. 23). We must read on in Romans 8:1-2 where such a person (including Paul) through a vital relationship with Jesus Christ becomes a "new creation" <u>able to repent, overcome and be free from the law of sin</u>. The "old man" in us will try to lead us to believe that if Paul can be this weak, void of self-control, and this much under the dominion of sin, so can we! This is looking for and embracing a fatal loophole to continue in our sin made possible by "easy believism" theology allowing us to interpret a scripture in a certain way because <u>we want</u> it that way and it seems right in our own eyes. If this happens to you, please pray to God as to what scriptures Peter was talking about in 2 Peter 3:14-15.

Don Z. Weldon

# REPENT AND OVERCOME

| TURN FROM AND OVERCOME THESE THINGS | REWARDS |
|---|---|
| * Church of Ephesus<br>Leaving and forsaking your first love (Me and My Ways)<br>Repent, do thy first works<br>Rev. 2:4-5 | To him that overcometh will I give to eat of the tree of life, which is in the midst of the paradise of God.<br>Rev. 2:7 |
| * Church of Smyrna<br>Do not fold with persecution<br>Rev. 2:10 | I will give thee a crown of life. He that overcometh shall not be hurt of the second death.<br>Rev. 2:10-11 |
| * Church of Pergamos<br>Tolerance of and indulgence in evil (food sacrificed unto idols, fornication, and holding the doctrine of the Nicolaitans)<br>Rev. 2:14-15 | I will give to eat of the hidden manna, and will give him a new name written. Rev. 2:17 (see church of Philadelphia below). |
| * Church of Sardis<br>Looking and sounding good but you are spiritually dead cold with imperfect works<br>Rev. 3:1-2 | He that overcometh, the same shall be clothed in white raiment, and I will not blot out his name out of the book of life, but I will confess his name before my father, and before his angels.<br>Rev. 3:5 |
| * Church of Philadelphia<br>Potentially losing the little spiritually you have. Hold fast which thou hast, that no man take thy crown<br>Rev. 3:11 | Him that overcometh will I make a pillar in the temple of my God, and he shall go no more out: and I will write upon him the name of my God, and the name of the city of my God, which is new Jerusalem, which cometh down out of heaven from my God: and I will write upon him my new name.<br>Rev. 3:12 |
| * Church of Laodicea<br>Your works indicate you are spiritually lukewarm and you are to be spewed out of the Lord's mouth. Realize spiritual depravity, genuinely respond to His promptings, insure that He comes into your heart and life. Be spiritually "hot" and intensely pursue the Lord and live His righteousness.<br>Rev. 3:15-20 | To him that overcometh will I grant to sit with me in my throne even as I also overcame, and am set down with my Father in his throne.<br>Rev. 3:21 |

Let's be spiritually reasonable and honest with ourselves and each other. Paul obviously had become a Spirit-filled "new creation". Otherwise, if he had been as spiritually flimsy as this "old man" description, he would not have been successful at all in "running the race," fighting the good fight, enduring and overcoming the incredible suffering as he was obedient to his calling and providing the earth with his divinely inspired New Testament scriptures. Romans 8:2 is the real "new creation" Paul.

## GOD'S GRACE

One of the many powers that God provides to His true converts is an unmerited favor "gift" that comes from God and is encapsulated in the marvelous provision called God's "grace." Consult <u>Strong's Exhaustive Concordance of the Bible</u> and you will find that the meaning of God's grace takes on an expanded definition after the coming of Jesus Christ. There is a power to change in "grace" that is expanded from the "unmerited favor" grace of the Old Testament. Grace in the New Testament is defined as an unmerited favor spiritual gift (act) of God for divine influence upon the heart and its reflection in the life. Much of the power that enables us to crucify our sin tendencies and truly follow Him and His ways comes from His gift of grace to us.

### Romans 6:14

> For sin shall not have dominion over you: for ye are not under the law, but under grace.

When we truly believe in Jesus Christ and ask Him to come into our lives (and truly open the door to Him) and abide in us and call on Him and confess Him as <u>our</u> Lord and Master, then we shall be saved. With His grace, we will be delivered from being under the "dominion of sin" and begin becoming a "new creation" (repentance and overcoming). We will be in the process of becoming a servant of righteousness.

*Don Z. Weldon*

# BECOMING A NEW CREATION

If we are truly saved, we will have a heart of repentance and a gift of powerful grace. Simultaneously we shall receive Christ's "imputed" (KJV) "credited" (NIV) righteousness into our lives.

## Romans 4:5

But to him that worketh not, but believeth on him that justifieth the ungodly, his faith is counted for righteousness.

## Romans 4:6

Even as David also describeth the blessedness of the man, unto whom God imputeth righteousness without works,

## James 2:20-24

But wilt thou know, O vain man, that faith without works is dead? [21] Was not Abraham our father justified by works, when he had offered Isaac his son upon the altar? [22] Seest thou how faith wrought with his works, and by works was faith made perfect? [23] And the scripture was fulfilled which saith, Abraham believed God, and it was imputed unto him for righteousness: and he was called the Friend of God. [24] Ye see then how that by works a man is justified, and not by faith only.

The words in prayers or stated requests and commitments to be saved must not come from just lips, vocal chords and a mind. They must also come from a genuinely convicted, sorrowful repentant heart and grateful, teachable <u>soul</u>.

With Christ abiding in us, we will then have the desire and ability to change and we will change becoming a new creation. We will begin to love the Lord, His Words and others that we couldn't love before. 2 Cor. 5:17 says: "Therefore if any man be in Christ, he is a new creature: old things are passed away; <u>behold</u>, all things are become new."

From working with a Christian counseling center, several discipleship seminars in the church, personally having a home ministry, weekly prayer fellowships or helping restore many marriages that were severely broken, WE <u>BEHELD</u> many <u>old things passing away</u> and many <u>new</u>

things "becoming new" as defeated believers became new genuine born again repentant Lordship Believers. Notice the strong presence of "repentance" (turning from "…and turning to…") in becoming a new creation.

* A bitter person can become gentle, kind and peaceful.

* An immoral person can become pure in thoughts and action.

* An angry person (reported to be the biggest problem of "most Christians") can become peaceful, calm, gentle, compassionate and loving.

* An unforgiving person can become forgiving and reconciliatory.

* A person under the dominion of willful, rampant, and defiant sin can become obedient to the Lord's Word and His promptings to his soul.

* A negligent, confused frustrated father can become a strong spiritual leader of the home winning the hearts of his children and inspiring them to genuine salvation, obedience and righteousness.

* A cold, selfish or abusive husband can change to a loving, sensitive wise leader inspiring a radiant responsiveness in his wife.

* A person caught up in emotional adultery and in a powerful mind, will, and emotions dominating snare of an affair can turn from this and heal his marriage.

* A lukewarm or cold marriage can become a marriage of great joy, happiness and fulfillment.

You might be asking "How can this be?! These are radical changes. I'm a Christian and I have tried some of these changes and I can't do it." The answer is, you are right – YOU can't! However, you can with His power if you are a genuine Lordship Christian and you believe that God indwelling you and His power can change you.

## Philip. 4:13

I can do all things through Christ which strengtheneth me.

## John 15:5

> I am the vine, ye are the branches: He that abideth in me, and I in him, the same bringeth forth much fruit: for without me ye can do nothing.

First and foremost, a person desiring to successfully repent and overcome must do their own personal salvation conversion right.

## SPIRITUAL CYCLES

Israel went through many cycles of spiritual incline and victory, and then spiritual decline and defeat. We are in the process of the latter. What can be done to turn this around? As always the answers are in the wonderful Bible. The power comes from Almighty God.

America's (and many other nation's) spiritual decline crises parallel that of Israel back when Jesus came to the earth. America's solutions need to come the same way as then.

Israel's spiritual, family and social conditions were pitiful. They didn't have the character or spiritual savvy to keep from murdering the Son of God. Evidently part of the problem was that parent child relationships hadn't improved since Malachi 4:6 was written and the nation had received the "curse" promised by God. God even allowed them to be under a foreign invader – Rome.

John (the Baptist) came to prepare people to turn to the Lord their God and to help them become obedient, wise and just. Part of this mission was to help restore family brokenness. It is extremely interesting as to what Godly parents he had and that his main message to accomplish these objectives was wrapped up in the word "REPENT". "Repentance" also encapsulates Jesus' message then and now.

## Luke 1:6

> And they (John's parents) were both righteous before God, walking in all the commandments and ordinances of the Lord blameless.

## Luke 1:16

And many of the children of Israel shall he turn to the Lord their God.

## Luke 1:17

And he shall go before him in the spirit and power of Elias, (1) <u>to turn the hearts of the fathers to the children</u>, (2) and the <u>disobedient to the wisdom of the just</u>; to make ready a people prepared for the Lord. (Notice the interconnection or interaction between 1 & 2.)

## Matthew 3:1-2

In those days came John the Baptist, preaching in the wilderness of Judaea, [2] And saying, Repent ye: for the kingdom of heaven is at hand.

## Matthew 4:17

From that time Jesus began to preach, and to say, Repent: for the kingdom of heaven is at hand.

## Luke 13:3

I tell you, Nay: but, except ye repent, ye shall all likewise perish.

# BROKEN FAMILIES

God despises divorce, circumstances leading to divorce, parents failing to raise Godly children, and broken parent-child relationships.

## Malachi 2:13-16

And this have ye done again, covering the altar of the Lord with tears, with weeping, and with crying out, insomuch that he regardeth not the offering any more, or receiveth it with good will at your hand.

[14] Yet ye say, Wherefore? Because the Lord hath been witness between thee and the wife of thy youth, against whom thou hast dealt treacherously: yet is she thy companion, and the wife of thy

covenant. [15] And did not he make one? Yet had he the residue of the spirit. And wherefore one? <u>That he might seek a godly seed (child)</u>. Therefore take heed to your spirit, and let none deal treacherously against the wife of his youth. [16] For the Lord, the God of Israel, saith that he <u>hateth</u> putting away (divorce): for one covereth violence with his garment, saith the Lord of hosts: therefore take heed to your spirit, that ye deal not treacherously.

## Malachi 4:6

And he shall turn the heart of the fathers to the children, and the heart of the children to their fathers, lest I come and smite the earth with a curse.

We must restore our broken or non-existent relationships between ourselves and God, between husbands and wives, and parents and children. It is very difficult to restore any one of these if the others are broken. The solutions can best come when there are simultaneous improvements in all these areas. This is the purpose of all this material. The success and survival of a nation ultimately depends upon God's blessings and the building block of a society – the home where the Lord is LORD!

## LEARNING AND DOING WHAT THE LORD SAYS

Christ did not come to earth so that He could just save us from our sins after we believe in Him. He came also to save us from sinning! We will not be able to become "sinless" but we will sin less and less if we believe in Him and mature in our faith the way He requires.

Right after John wrote:

1 John 1:8 If we say that we have no sin, we deceive ourselves, and the truth is not in us.

… the Lord inspired him to write some rather remarkable strong assertions regarding what should happen to a person who becomes a true follower of Jesus Christ. Apparently John is reflecting on the true nature of man – that he is a free-will being even after he is saved. There is no way we could become sinless as was Jesus. However, our

Lord apparently is saying to us that if we more and more love Him and respond to His promptings and His Word (obedience) we will increasingly become willing volunteer servants of righteousness (as Paul described). With Christ indwelling us as our Master, more and more our free will comes in line with His will (hearing and doing what He says) enabling us to increasingly subdue and defeat our sin tendencies and live His truth and light.

"Grievous" in the following scripture means not too burdensome, not too hard for us.

## 1 John 5:3-5

> For this is the love of God, that <u>we keep his commandments: and his commandments are not grievous</u>. [4] For whatsoever is born of God overcometh the world: and this is the victory that overcometh the world, even our faith. [5] <u>Who is he that overcometh the world, but he that believeth that Jesus is the Son of God?</u>

## 1 John 2:1-6

> My little children, these things write I unto you, that ye sin not. And if any man sin, we have an advocate with the Father, Jesus Christ the righteous: [2] And he is the propitiation for our sins: and not for ours only, but also for the sins of the whole world. [3] And hereby we do know that we know him, if we keep his commandments. [4] <u>He that saith, I know him, and keepeth not his commandments, is a liar, and the truth is not in him.</u> [5] But whoso keepeth his word, in him verily is the love of God perfected: hereby know we that we are in him. [6] He that saith he abideth in him ought himself also so to walk, even as he walked.

## 1 John 2:17

> And the world passeth away, and the lust thereof: but <u>he that doeth the will of God abideth for ever.</u>

## Matthew 7:21

Not every one that saith unto me, Lord, Lord, shall enter into the kingdom of heaven; <u>but he that doeth the will of my Father</u> which is in heaven.

## 1 John 3:6

<u>Whosoever abideth in him sinneth not</u>: whosoever sinneth hath not seen him, neither known him.

## 1 John 3:9-10

<u>Whosoever is born of God doth not commit sin</u>; for his seed remaineth in him: and he cannot sin, because he is born of God. [10] In this the children of God are manifest, and the children of the devil: <u>whosoever doeth not righteousness is not of God, neither he that loveth not his brother.</u>

## 1 John 3:24

And <u>he that keepeth his commandments dwelleth in him, and he in him</u>. And hereby we know that he abideth in us, by the Spirit which he hath given us.

## 1 John 4:15-16

<u>Whosoever shall confess that Jesus is the Son of God, God dwelleth in him</u>, and <u>he in God</u>. [16] And we have known and believed the love that God hath to us. God is love; and he that dwelleth in love dwelleth in God, and God in him.

## 1 John 4:18

There is no fear in love; but perfect love casteth out fear: because fear hath torment. He that feareth is not made perfect in love.

## 1 John 4:4

<u>Ye are of God</u>, little children, and <u>have overcome them: because greater is he that is in you, than he that is in the world.</u>

Again, the main message we must not miss here is that salvation and righteousness are <u>extremely</u> interconnected. Just making some statements of believing in Jesus and asking Him to come into your life won't work if you don't truly let Him and His Word and ways become part of you and affect everything you become and do.

This is not under any analysis, salvation because of what you do (works). You are saved through the blood sacrifice of Jesus Christ, His grace and a relationship with Him. It is however, if you truly appreciate and respond appropriately to His sacrifice and accept Him indwelling your life as your Lord and Master, you will do all sorts of righteous works or deeds as His Spirit guides your life from within. If you do not do righteous deeds, according to His promptings, or from obedience to His Word, or exhibit His fruit of the Spirit, or continue in habitual and defiant unrighteousness, then this is a strong indication that Jesus has not been able to enter and guide your life. You are on very thin ice regarding a relationship with Him and with your eternal destiny. The abiding Jesus always changes people and inspires righteousness.

If you are presently in what some call a spiritual "backslidden" condition, but feel you are still saved, you also are on very thin ice. You might not have ever established Jesus as your indwelling Lord, Master, and Savior. When you are confronted with the "words of the kingdom" you might have "hard packed, stony or thorny ground" responses and you might have done your conversion wrong.

## Galatians 5:24

And they that are Christ's have crucified the flesh with the affections and lusts.

## Romans 8:9

But ye are not in the flesh, but in the Spirit, if so be that the Spirit of God dwell in you. **Now if any man have not the Spirit of Christ, he is none of his.**

Our Lord says the most important scripture in the Bible is for us to intensely love Him. (Matt. 22:37) He did not say the most important was to believe in Him or call on Him. (If we intensely love Him we will do this right.) This has major impact as to how we live. Jesus says those who love Him keep His commandments. Loving the Lord is the major ingredient in a successful relationship with Him and is most critical in our ability to forsake our darkness (repent) and become new creations. Only through the presence and practice of this scripture in our lives can the other scriptures become truly life-changing.

We can't overemphasize the necessity of transforming the power of this principle into our family relationships. Children who truly love their parents are very prone to "keep" their commandments. If we are Lordship Christians and can win and keep the hearts of our children enabling them to love us dearly, we provide them with the most important gifts we can ever give them – the ability to enthusiastically practice compliant obedience to our Lord inspired requirements and wishes (Eph. 6:1-3, Ex. 20:12). This will go a long way to predispose them to develop and maintain a teachable spirit regarding our training and the Lord's direct training to our children of the ways of God .

## Isaiah 54:13

> And all thy children shall be taught of the Lord; and great shall be the peace of thy children.

If we genuinely love God and we are obedient to His calling for us to love Him and keep His commandments and we have won and kept the hearts of our children, they will see the benefits and blessings and become extremely prone to love and obey Him also.

Teenage rebellion is more of a learned expected cultural thing. It doesn't have to happen! We have experienced this personally in our family, observed it in many other families, and learned of it in other societies.

Spouses need to work at keeping each other's hearts also. The resultant blessings and rewards of successfully doing this are indescribably delicious and it goes a long way in meeting one of the greatest needs of our children – for the parents to love each other.

## SOME PULPIT ERRORS

How awesomely unfortunate it is that many of our spiritual leaders at the conclusion of an intense Holy Spirit inspired teaching and preaching session trying with all their heart to motivate the listeners to stop a particular sin or adopt and live some righteous principle(s) end the messages or have a highly frequent theological statement in other messages, that <u>destroys the slightest motivation</u> that the listeners might have to putting the sermon or lesson to practice in their lives, to evaluate their relationship with the Lord, to repent, or to become a new creation. Possibly the strongest motivation of a "believer" is to take care of the heaven and eternity issues.

One way or the other, the speaker tragically assures the listeners that they really do not have to become or do what he preached about because as long as they have prayed or said the "gold standard commitments" they are "saved". They have no other requirements. Jesus paid it all. THEY HAVE TO "PAY" NOTHING BUT A BELIEF STATEMENT.

This gives the strong impression that our righteous living and obedience to God is optional, unnecessary or undesirable because it reeks of "salvation by works" or "legalism". We're sorry if this causes stress and discomfort, but we must point out that this theology is the backbone of easy believism and fatal loophole religious reasoning.

## SUMMARY – EASY BELIEVISM CHRISTIANITY – DOING OUR CONVERSION WRONG

Here is what a typical gold standard scriptures only "christian" that has a soul that has hard packed, stony or thorny ground can believe, become and do:

   * He prays or commits to receive Christ into his heart but in his self-will keeps Jesus out. He is a listener and "learner" but not a becomer and a doer. He talks the talk but doesn't walk the walk.

   * He says he believes or actually believes in Jesus Christ but wants Him as His future Savior from hell only or as a way to get to heaven.

He does not presently want Jesus as His Lord and Master or to do what He says.

* He believes that all his past, present and future sins are forever forgiven and forgotten and this frees him to remain his old self, sinning all he wants to.

* His lukewarm profession of faith or prayer to receive Christ came from his mind, lips and vocal cords, not from his heart and soul.

* He is incapable of true repentance and cannot defeat his lifetime of favorite sins, iniquities and worldly pleasures and pursuits.

* He has no fear of offending God or being disobedient to His Word or promptings

* He does not love Jesus and His light or others the way Jesus requires.

* He loves and lives his darkness, does not become a new creation and thereby is a condemned professed "believer" but is really an unbeliever according to John 3:16-20 that is unsaved and will perish.

## SUMMARY – LORDSHIP CHRISTIANITY – DOING OUR CONVERSION RIGHT

Here is what a "good ground", born again, God-loving, God-honoring Christian typically believes, becomes and does. The gold standard scriptures are an essential starting point to his salvation. He goes further with the Lord and:

* He unequivocally invites and welcomes Jesus and His ways to come into his heart and life.

* He believes his past, present and future sins are forgiven and forgotten and with Jesus' indwelling he increasingly is able to sin less and less.

* He loves the Lord intensely and is divinely enabled to genuinely love others.

\* He believes such that he is obedient to Jesus. Jesus is his <u>Lord</u> and <u>Master</u>. His conversion request and commitment came from his heart and soul.

\* He has a spirit of repentance in his relationship with the Lord and is enabled to turn from sins and iniquities to truth and light.

\* He has a teachable heart to the ways of God.

\* He is genuinely thankful to the Lord for His sacrifice.

\* He becomes a new creation as he makes progress to crucify his sin nature and become a servant of righteousness. He does this through the power of grace in his life, and learning and living the Lord's Words.

\* HE IS ENGAGED HEAVILY IN COMMUNICATING WITH THE LORD THROUGH HIS WORD, PRAYER AND DETECTING HIS PROMPTINGS.

\* He develops a positive "healthy" fear of the Lord that enriches his faith and obedience to His Word and promptings.

\* He is a <u>non-condemned</u> believer and will not perish because he is attracted to and loves Jesus and His light, lives His truth and his observable deeds come from his spirit engaged and cooperating with the Lord.

## John 3:21

> But he that doeth truth cometh to the light, that his deeds may be made manifest, that they are wrought in God.

## Romans 8:1-2

> There is therefore now no condemnation to them which are in Christ Jesus, who walk not after the flesh, but after the Spirit. [2] For the law of the Spirit of life in Christ Jesus hath made me free from the law of sin and death.

To some, this will sound too much, too complicated, and too hard. Worthy of some concern, some soul searching and maybe some worry is the statement by Christ:

## Matthew 7:13-14

> Enter ye in at the strait gate: for wide is the gate, and broad is the way, that leadeth to destruction, and many there be which go in thereat: [14] Because strait is the gate, and narrow is the way, which leadeth unto life, and <u>few there be that find it.</u>

## FORSAKING EASY BELIEVISM

Unfortunately there is yet another vast contributor to the masses of unsaved believers. It is disconcerting enough that it will be met with an understandable degree of discomfort and possible indignation.

This contributor comes from incomplete follow-through on the Great Commission. Note that the new converts are to be taught to keep Christ's commandments.

## Matthew 28:19-20

> Go ye therefore, and teach all nations, baptizing them in the name of the Father, and of the Son, and of the Holy Ghost: [20] Teaching them to observe <u>all things</u> whatsoever I have commanded you: and, lo, I am with you alway, even unto the end of the world. Amen.

In verse 19, we are commanded to be a part of God's plan to bring new followers into the kingdom of God. From this requirement we have developed a fairly comfortable process whereby we are to be obedient to verse 19, but the process enables us to severely fall short on verse 20. We have determined that we are to present the gospel (process to become converted) but have determined that it is God's power and responsibility to "save them". This is true but…

We feel that once we have seen and heard that the new convert prays to receive Christ and says the commitments of salvation, our job is done and we can go on to the next convert. This is not exactly compatible with verse 20.

If our gospel that we present is laced with "easy believism" and so is the church that the new convert might get "plugged into", the chances are quite high that the conversion and the discipleship will go awry.

For example, a survey showed that an intensive evangelistic campaign yielded over 200,000 converts but later only 10% showed up in a church exhibiting their faith.

It seems very apparent in scripture that those doing the evangelism must either personally teach the converts to observe all things whatsoever Christ has commanded, or go to <u>great lengths</u> to insure that someone else does. There are not "all things" Christ commanded us to observe in this package of materials, but there is a lot of <u>very critical</u> "things" that will help a person, family or church become and do (observe) these and the other "all things".

Professed Christians all over our land are growing cold and becoming spiritual "dropouts" "because their faith is not working for them". It will if they will become Lordship Christians!

If we continue or even increase our spiritual business as usual in the churches, embracing easy believism, we will never be able to turn around the situations where the average lukewarm believer turns other people off to Christianity. With the humanistic public education, entertainment and news media, there will be continued or increasing unrighteous disobedience to God's ways by average lukewarm believers and non Christians bringing increasing destruction to families including neglect, abuse, affairs, divorce, and wild, independent rebellious children. Marriages will continue to fail in the churches as fast as those outside the churches. We will continue to lose 80% of the children raised in the churches "to the world" by the age of 26, and some project Christianity will be a minority religion by 2020. We most likely will never have a revival or spiritual awakening. Christianity could potentially become voted or legislated into becoming a "remnant".

These situations must be turned around. There must be a massive turning to righteousness in the land by "believers" who become genuine, born again, Lordship Christians who have let the indwelling Lord be <u>their</u> Lord and Master – learning, becoming and doing what He says.

Through preaching and teaching, we must and can persuade believers to do this since <u>there is such strong scriptural evidence that if a person is really interested in going to heaven, Lordship Christianity is a</u>

requirement. Any contrasting resistant theological system of belief to Lordship Christianity has a greater chance of being wrong in God's eyes since it would most likely grant its followers greater freedom to sin and feel comfortable with it. With Lordship Christianity, Believers will much more be motivated to "trust, believe and obey, for there is no other way!"

Families in churches can again return to the even lower divorce rate of the 1970's when it was reported that only 1 marriage in 1100 failed among Christians when the couples regularly attended church together, read the Bible together and prayed together.

We must quit undermining and destroying believers' motivation to repent and overcome and become new creations by constantly assuring them that their heavenly destiny is assured if they just said the basic commitments of belief and faith. We must let them know that they can do their conversion experience wrong.

As mentioned earlier, let's minimize the endless winless war on the symptoms of the problem, (massive unrighteousness) by believers, swallow our doctrinal pride, and maximize the war on the causes of the problem ("easy believism" and believers not becoming new creations).

Incidentally, our information is very limited on this, but we have heard of a foreign church expanding into a new region coming up with a unique program to deal with the negative impact on church growth of lukewarm, counterfeit, unloving or misbehaving "Christians". They developed an intensive discipleship program that lasted a year making sure the new converts became, what sounded like, Lordship Christians before they could formally join the membership. Those that were insincere and uninterested in truly following the Lord and CONTINUED living in darkness evidently dropped out thereby eliminating them from giving the church or Christianity a bad image. There might be something here worth considering.

## ADDING POWER TO YOUR PRAYERS

Families and individuals can be blindsided by some undesirable personal qualities or problems, and bad behavior (or diseases) that can pop up at various ages as a result of the inherited potential from four generations of forefathers. At least one or more persons in this genealogy most likely will have "hated" the Lord.

### Exodus 20:5

> Thou shalt not bow down thyself to them, nor serve them: for I the Lord thy God am a jealous God, <u>visiting the iniquity of the fathers upon the children</u> unto the third and fourth generation of them that hate me;

To reduce or counteract this bondage to a possible "visitation" to you or your family or as part of your regular prayer time issues, consider praying something along these lines:

"Heavenly Father, realizing that in addition to my own sin nature and shortcomings, many of my problems have their origin from Satan and his followers, I pray that you help me to be strong in you, Lord, and in the power of Your might. I pray that YOU bind and rebuke Satan (Jude 1:9, Eph. 6:12), his principalities and powers, rulers of the darkness, and spiritual wickedness in high places from my life (and/or other people and issues)."

"Realizing I can have some capabilities and responsibilities in this process, I put on the whole armor of God (MAKE SURE THIS IS TRUE) to stand against the wiles of the devil – the helmet of salvation, the breastplate of righteousness, the shield of faith, the sword of the Spirit, the belt of truth, and the gospel of peace on my feet. (Please read Eph. 6:10-17.)"

"I do this in the precious name of my Lord, Jesus Christ, the power of His blood sacrificed for me and the victory of His finished work on the cross. I have the authority to bind and rebuke you, Satan, and your followers, and you have to leave me and/or (---) alone because <u>it is written</u> that greater is He (the Lord) that is in me than he that is in the world (Satan) – (1 John 4:4). It is also written that I can resist you and you will flee from me. (James 4:7) My Lord resisted and defeated you and your temptations with "it is written" statements from the powerful Holy Scriptures and you were defeated and departed from Him (Matt. 4:4-11)."*

Asking God to guide you, look up words in a concordance for "it is written" scriptures related to your problems and temptations or those of others you are praying for. For example, in intercessory prayer for others, Mark 2:8-5 has a great "for it is written" statement. When Jesus saw the <u>earnestness and FAITH of those helping the sick man, Jesus healed him</u>!

"I pray, Heavenly Father, that you will help me defeat a "visit" of any inherited and personal weakness problems (or others being prayed for). I pray that you enable me to let You indwell me so mightily that I have access to whichever of Your attributes I especially need and You will share with me in areas such as unconditional love, endurance, peace, joy, wisdom, power, self-control (others).

> \* I pray that I can be free from ANY bondage to sin habits and iniquities of my forefathers and those of my own making,
>
> \* I pray that I can be free from any bondage to inherited potential diseases and those of my own making through lack of self control, neglecting health and nutrition principles
>
> \* I pray that I can be delivered from any bondage to inherited offensive personality quirks, and hang-ups, and character shortcomings and flaws and those of my own making.

Guide and help me to have these victories from Your indwelling power and the power of your Word and grace in my life, the power of prayer, the power of rebuking and resisting Satan, the power of putting and keeping on the full armor of God and the power of knowing You and Your truth which will set me free (Jo.8:32,38) to become the new creation I want to be and that You desire. I pray these things in the name of Jesus Christ.

Amen."

---

\* Significant portions of this are from the Institute in Basic Life Principles.

# CONCLUSIONS

As in Jeremiah's day, America, (and American Christianity) is living in the <u>crosshairs</u> of many external <u>and</u> internal enemies. Many of our most determined internal enemies are prominent influential citizens doggedly determined to make America what seems right in their own eyes – not what scripture says is right for a nation to be God blessed and protected.

In Genesis 18, we find how God feels about righteousness. When God was prepared to destroy a city because of the extent of their unrighteousness, He promised Abraham that He would not destroy the city if He could find between 10 and 50 <u>righteous</u> men in the city. God could not and the city was destroyed!

Even in the last days prior to the "Second Coming", God's emphasis on righteous living is evident to His followers.

### 2 Peter 3:3

> Knowing this first, that there shall come in the last days scoffers, walking after their own lusts,

### 2 Peter 3:11

> Seeing then that all these things shall be dissolved, what manner of persons ought ye to be in all holy conversation and godliness,

### 2 Peter 3:14

> Wherefore, beloved, seeing that ye look for such things, be diligent that ye may be found of him in peace, without spot, and blameless.

What is the response to these neglected and misinterpreted scriptures by those professing to be Christians and believe in the Bible? Will it be as in Jeremiah's day?

### Jeremiah 18:11-12

> Now therefore go to, speak to the men of Judah, and to the inhabitants of Jerusalem, saying, Thus saith the Lord; Behold, I frame evil against you, and devise a device against you: return ye

now every one from his evil way, and make your ways and your doings good. [12] And they said, THERE IS <u>NO HOPE</u>: but we will walk after our own devices, and we will every one do the imagination of his evil heart.

There was indeed no hope and God allowed the enemies to "pull the trigger" and the people lost their nation and were destroyed or taken into captivity.

Will American spiritual leaders and members respond, "There is no hope! We are in bondage to the scriptures we embrace and cannot change our behavior or consider or bring about change in our system of creating 'followers' of Christ. Repenting and overcoming is beyond our capabilities!"?

We believe that since these neglected Lordship scriptures are in the Bible there is hope that we can "repent and overcome".

We believe that Americans can and have changed when it was shown that our future was truly at stake. It will do so in the present and future. It seems very plausible that THE VARIOUS DENOMINATIONS, WITH PRAYER AND GOD'S HELP CAN AT LEAST RALLY THEIR SALVATION PLANS AROUND THESE SCRIPTURES AND HAVE A COMMON OBJECTIVE TO CREATE TRULY SAVED AND MORE RIGHTEOUS MEMBERSHIPS!

Let us change our easy believism mindset that we have a whole life-time to get our spiritual act together. Let's let Christ powerfully abide in us, have His way in us becoming Lordship Christians rapidly during conversion or shortly thereafter, and many of us can avoid ruining our families and our future. It is highly unlikely that two true born-again, abiding in the Lord, new creation, Lordship followers of Jesus Christ can entertain affairs, divorce, abuse and neglect in their family. Also, the earlier we can do this, the more the certainty that we can avoid rebellious, independent, wild children, because it will be more likely that we can "win and keep their hearts" and enable the Lord to do likewise.

Let's quit being an embarrassment to our Lord and a mockery to His Holy name. Let's quit <u>thinking of ourselves, giving ourselves</u>

<u>permission, and living</u> as if we are "dirty rotten sinners saved by grace" (a popular term in some Christian circles). Let's become <u>new creations</u> in line with <u>God's will</u> – very successful in being holy, righteous and good because we are saved by grace! We should be highly motivated to do this since there are undeniable scriptural indications that our heavenly eternal destiny is riding on us having an effective powerful relationship with Jesus that will help us crucify our sin nature and grow in righteousness.

Let's completely terminate the likelihood that because of us, someone would say, "I'd become a Christian if it weren't for Christians" and give ample reasons for them to say "I want to become a Christian because of what I observe in Christians."

This book is not by any pretense an all inclusive guidance package of building and maintaining good relationships with our Lord, our spouses, our children and others. Look at these scriptures and principles therein as highlights and very basic insights, which if understood and adopted, will enable you to become and do the other things in God's Word to attain a strong and successful Christ-built home on earth and in heaven.

This project is a call for national repentance especially by God's people who are called by His name. In the twentieth century there was a gradual migration in our society away from the ways of God and the momentum has been accelerating at the end of the century and beginning of the twenty-first century.

As godliness has declined, godlessness has rushed in to take its place. Currently, godlessness is pushing godliness out.

Repentance is much more than feeling sorry for our sins and/or confessing them. It is turning from them and overcoming them. It is also turning back to God's ways which is absolutely essential to the survival of our culture, our churches, our political system, our families, and inspiring God to bless and protect America.

Very high on our Lord's hierarchy of requirements is for us to be righteous generations reproducing righteous generations from godly righteous homes! In this we are falling woefully short!

Don Z. Weldon

From years of concerns with these matters, we have compiled for your consideration non-denominational scriptural answers as to what are the problems, what causes the problems, how to solve the problems, and very importantly, how to <u>motivate</u> God's people to overcome the problems.

If we are to truly accommodate Christ's "Great Commission" (Matt. 28:19-20) to create true disciples who <u>observe His teachings</u> (Matt. 7:21, Luke 6:46), we must make some significant adjustments in our theologies regarding leading a person to the all important decision to become a Christian and then to grow as a Christian. The typical plan of salvation scriptures and the supportive persuasions are void of any repentance or personal commitments to grow in righteousness after becoming a Christian. Much of hearing a lifetime of preaching and teaching supports this.

Obedience to principles of righteousness are taught in discipleship basically as <u>recommendations</u> leading to consequential blessings, and/or as merely the <u>desires</u> of a merciful, loving, tolerant and forgetful God - all of which leads many "believers" to conclude that righteous living is a minimally important option after becoming saved.

Obviously a minority of Believers grow past this into a reasonable degree of righteous holy living. The majority obviously does not, leading to personal "earthly" and "eternal" disasters. It seems quite obvious why we have so many lukewarm believers and spiritual drop outs who decide that their faith is not working for them and in others they observe.

The first of the "significant adjustments" is in the initial conversion to become a Christian. In the salvation or conversion process, we need to greater predispose and encourage the new converts to truly following the Lord (becoming a Lordship Christian).

Let's strongly consider adding some more scriptural principles regarding salvation to their commitments (or sinner's prayer) of faith and belief to become a Christian:

> \* **I ask you, Lord, to come into my life and I wholeheartedly welcome You to come in as Lord and Master of my life.**

* **I will learn of Your ways from the Bible and will do my utmost to obey your teachings.**

* **I am sorry for my sins, confess them to you and in repentance, with Your help, turn from, forsake, and overcome them, and as quickly as possible begin to become the new creation You want me to be.**

* **With all the strength of my being, in compliance to Your #1 commandment, I will purpose to love you more and more, which will empower me to do Your will and to love and treat others as You desire. (John 14:23, 1 John 3:10)**

* **I will grow in my personal relationship with You and serve You in an assembly of other like-spirited Believers (Heb. 10:22-25) that preach and live Your word.**

Obviously, the wording needs to be different for children, keeping the concepts as close as possible.

(We are confident this will not scare off too many new converts as we have recently discovered that much of the above is included in the preaching and salvation commitments of one of America's largest churches.)

The stronger we love our husbands or wives, the greater the desire and ability to keep the wedding vows. The stronger we love Jesus, the greater our desire and ability to keep His commandments. Interestingly, the more we love Jesus and His commands, and truly let Him in, the greater our desire and ability through His power and wisdom to keep the wedding vows and to reproduce godly generations.

The author of No Believer Left Behind is of the middle age - seniors segment of our society. This group which is massive must strongly consider that we were very, very fortunate to have inherited a strong God blessed America. We owe it to those who preceded us, many of which died to preserve our religious freedoms and our country, to wake up and try to mend what has been undone during the twentieth century. If the Lord's second coming is imminent, that's wonderful! However, since we do not know how long our Lord will tarry in this, we owe it to our sons, daughters and grandchildren to inherit and enjoy what was provided for us. The best way for there to be a God blessed America in the future is for us to have a revival and spiritual awakening very soon. No, not a "revival" of what existed in the recent past but a revival of the prevailing spiritual excellence of our founding fathers when they formulated our nation with Almighty God's help and blessings. We can do this as we become a nation with greatly improved relationships between us and the Lord and within our families - a nation of righteous Believers raising righteous generations. To do this, "easy believism" must fade into history and massive turning to Lordship Christianity must become the spiritual state of the union.

## ALMOST PERSUADED? - 2006

Do you still feel that there is the slightest possibility that a Believer does not necessarily have to grow in righteousness after becoming "saved"?

Do you feel a need for scriptural indications as to whether you are really saved and will be counted among the godly righteous citizens of Heaven? Can you contribute to the numbers of righteous people inspiring God to bless, protect, spare, or "heal" a city or a nation? If your answer is "yes" to any of these, this is especially for you.

God does not and has not changed. He has required compliance to His commandments from Genesis to Revelation. The coming of Jesus and His salvation provision did not change this.

Through His coming, the Lord provided us with not only a heavenly eternal destiny and the forgiveness of sins, but also the guidance, desire and power to keep His commands which includes a decreasing propensity to sin against Him and others.

When things are looking bad, some Christians, perhaps the majority, prefer to choose to become nothing different, do nothing different, feeling and saying, "Relax, God is in control." Nothing you can do or we can do will affect anything! That's true to some extent! However, "His story" has shown that God exercises His control over His "people" in relation to the extent that they are <u>under His control</u> - a close, loving, obedient relationship, or out from under His control - a distant, disobedient, rebellious relationship. Obviously the appropriate time to relax is when we, our churches, our communities and our nation are under His control.

## Deut. 28:1-15

And it shall come to pass, if thou shalt <u>hearken diligently unto the voice of the Lord thy God, to observe and to do all his commandments</u> which I command thee this day, that the Lord thy God will set thee on high above all nations of the earth: [2] And all these blessings shall come on thee, and overtake thee, if thou shalt hearken unto the voice of the Lord thy God. [3] Blessed shalt thou be in the city, and blessed shalt thou be in the field. [4] Blessed shall be the fruit of thy body, and the fruit of thy ground, and the fruit of thy cattle, the increase of thy kine, and the flocks of thy sheep. [5] Blessed shall be thy basket and thy store. [6] Blessed shalt thou be when thou comest in, and blessed shalt thou be when thou goest out. [7] The Lord shall cause thine enemies that rise up against thee to be smitten before thy face: they shall come out against thee one way, and flee before thee seven ways. [8] The Lord shall command the blessing upon thee in thy storehouses, and in all that thou settest thine hand unto; and he shall bless thee in the land which the Lord thy God giveth thee. [9] The Lord shall establish thee an holy people unto himself, as he hath sworn unto thee, if thou shalt keep the commandments of the Lord thy God, and walk in his ways. [10] And all people of the earth shall see that thou art called by the name of the Lord; and they shall be afraid of thee. [11] And the Lord shall make thee plenteous in goods, in the fruit of thy body, and in the fruit of thy cattle, and in the fruit of thy ground, in the land which the Lord sware unto thy fathers to give thee. [12] The Lord shall open unto thee his good treasure, the heaven to give the rain unto thy land in his season, and to bless all the work of thine hand: and thou shalt lend unto many nations, and thou shalt not borrow. [13] And the Lord shall make thee the head, and not the tail; and thou shalt be above only, and thou shalt not be beneath; if that thou hearken unto the commandments of the Lord thy God, which I command thee this day, to observe and to do them: [14] And thou shalt not go aside from any of the words which I command thee this day, to the right hand, or to the left, to go after other gods to serve them.

[15] But it shall come to pass, if thou wilt not hearken unto the voice of the Lord thy God, to observe to do all his commandments

and his statutes which I command thee this day; that all these curses shall come upon thee, and overtake thee:

## Deut. 28:20-22

The Lord shall send upon thee cursing, vexation, and rebuke, in all that thou settest thine hand unto for to do, until thou be destroyed, and until thou perish quickly; because of the wickedness of thy doings, whereby thou hast forsaken me. [21] The Lord shall make the <u>pestilence cleave unto thee</u>, until he have <u>consumed thee from off the land</u>, whither thou goest to possess it. [22] The Lord shall <u>smite thee with a consumption, and with a fever</u>, and with an <u>inflammation</u>, and with an <u>extreme burning</u>, and with the <u>sword</u>, and with <u>blasting</u>, and <u>with mildew</u>; and they shall pursue thee until thou perish.

It's amazing how much these weapons (in 21 & 22) seem to be related to "weapons of mass destruction".

## Deut. 28:47-49

Because thou servedst not the Lord thy God with joyfulness, and with gladness of heart, for the abundance of all things; [48] Therefore shalt thou serve thine enemies which the Lord shall send against thee, in hunger, and in thirst, and in nakedness, and in want of all things: and he shall put a yoke of iron upon thy neck, until he have destroyed thee. [49] The Lord shall bring a nation against thee from far, from the end of the earth, as swift as the eagle flieth; a nation whose tongue thou shalt not understand;

## Psalm 127:1

EXCEPT THE LORD BUILD THE HOUSE, THEY LABOUR IN VAIN THAT BUILD IT: EXCEPT THE LORD KEEP THE CITY, THE WATCHMAN WAKETH BUT IN VAIN.

## Genesis 18:28

Peradventure there shall lack five of the fifty righteous: wilt thou destroy all the city for lack of five? And he said, If I find there forty and five, I will not destroy it.

## Genesis 18:32

And he said, Oh let not the Lord be angry, and I will speak yet but this once: Peradventure ten shall be found there. And he said, I will not destroy it for ten's sake.

## 2 Chron. 7:14

If my people, which are called by my name, shall humble themselves, and pray, and seek my face, and turn from their wicked ways; then will I hear from heaven, and will forgive their sin, and will heal their land.

## BELL CURVE POPULATION DISTRIBUTION

The population Bell Curve is a statistical tool promoting understanding as to how qualities are distributed in a grouping. In groups of people, for instance, intelligence, sports skills, musical skills, teaching skills, driving skills, incomes, attractiveness, etc. are unevenly distributed. In a Bell Curve distribution, some people (16%) possess none or a little, most people (68%) possess average amounts, and the remaining (16%) possess a lot. Righteousness is also roughly distributed in this fashion.

Symbolically, according to the Lord, people respond to the "seeds" (words of the kingdom – Matt. 13:3-23) with four different kinds of soil (souls) with differing harvests and/or fruits: <u>hard packed soil</u> yielding no roots, plant, or fruit, <u>rocky shallow soil</u> yielding a little root and a little plant that soon withers and dies producing no fruit, <u>thorny soil</u> that produces roots, a plant and some fruit that is inconsequential because it is choked out by overwhelming competition (worldly pursuits, temptations, pressures and circumstances), and <u>good soil</u> with good roots and a good plant producing much fruit. (Fruit is basically the person becoming and doing what the Lord says and helping others do likewise.)

"Easy believism" theology evidently has tragically produced this distribution of righteousness of those professing to be saved right in line with the Bell Curve. This whole set of materials is targeted to remedy this tragedy. <u>Easy believism evangelism and discipling produces a large group of spiritually cold and lukewarm Christians, neither of which are favorably looked upon by the Lord.</u> This will be covered later.

See the Bell Curve distribution of righteousness chart and scriptures on the next 5 pages. When studying this righteousness distribution chart, please do not get hung up on the exact percentage numbers. Just observe the parallels and meaning behind the percentage categories as they <u>generally</u> relate to righteousness. There is significant overlap and inexactness between the categories.

Recent church history and estimates by many evangelical leaders reveal that currently theology is creating between 50% and 80% of the church memberships being "lost" or "counterfeit" followers of the Lord and only 20% to 50% being genuinely "saved".

What happens to the lost person going through easy believism evangelism and discipling? Since there is little or no emphasis on a personal, powerful, loving, indwelling obedience relationship with Jesus Christ, and becoming righteous is optional, the person is pretty much left to his own devices and predispositions as to how he responds to his "believing" and "calling on the Lord" to be saved. Predominantly, there is little or no change in what he becomes and what he does.

Part of the hard packed, rocky and thorny souls' problem is a heart issue. In easy believism "conversions", while requesting salvation, a person can say or pray for Jesus to come into their heart and life but their strong self-will denies letting Him or His ways come in or have little or anything to do with their lives. EASY BELIEVISM THEOLOGY OR DOCTRINE GIVES A PERSON "PERMISSION" OR FREEDOM TO DO THIS. Possibly deep inside they intend to stay the boss or "lord" of their own lives for the rest of their lives. While requesting salvation a person can be serving the Lord with their lips, but their heart can be far (and stay far) from Him. There is much preaching and teaching <u>against unrighteousness</u> and <u>for righteousness</u> but accommodating these are not considered in easy believism to be "mandatory" requirements of the Lord.

## Matthew 15:8-9

> This people draweth nigh unto me with their mouth, and honoureth me with their lips; but their heart is far from me. [9] But in vain they do worship me, teaching for doctrines the commandments of men.

*No Believer Left Behind*

## BELL CURVE RIGHTEOUSNESS DISTRIBUTION

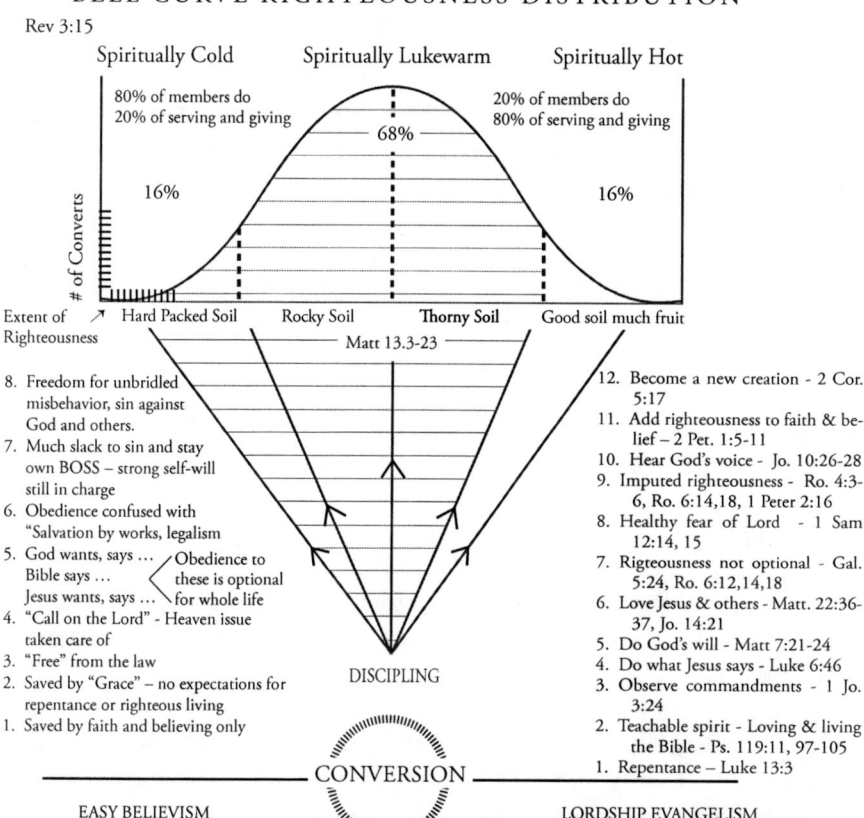

Rev 3:15

Spiritually Cold — Spiritually Lukewarm — Spiritually Hot

80% of members do 20% of serving and giving
68%
20% of members do 80% of serving and giving

16% — 16%

# of Converts

Extent of Righteousness — Hard Packed Soil — Rocky Soil — **Thorny Soil** — Good soil much fruit

Matt 13.3-23

8. Freedom for unbridled misbehavior, sin against God and others.
7. Much slack to sin and stay own BOSS – strong self-will still in charge
6. Obedience confused with "Salvation by works, legalism
5. God wants, says … / Obedience to
   Bible says … < these is optional
   Jesus wants, says … \ for whole life
4. "Call on the Lord" – Heaven issue taken care of
3. "Free" from the law
2. Saved by "Grace" – no expectations for repentance or righteous living
1. Saved by faith and believing only

12. Become a new creation - 2 Cor. 5:17
11. Add righteousness to faith & belief – 2 Pet. 1:5-11
10. Hear God's voice - Jo. 10:26-28
9. Imputed righteousness - Ro. 4:3-6, Ro. 6:14,18, 1 Peter 2:16
8. Healthy fear of Lord - 1 Sam 12:14, 15
7. Righteousness not optional - Gal. 5:24, Ro. 6:12,14,18
6. Love Jesus & others - Matt. 22:36-37, Jo. 14:21
5. Do God's will - Matt 7:21-24
4. Do what Jesus says - Luke 6:46
3. Observe commandments - 1 Jo. 3:24
2. Teachable spirit - Loving & living the Bible - Ps. 119:11, 97-105
1. Repentance – Luke 13:3

DISCIPLING

CONVERSION

EVANGELISM

LOST PERSON

### EASY BELIEVISM
### ROMANS ROAD TO SALVATION

Believe – Jesus is God's son – Jo. 3:16

Call on the Lord and be saved – Ro. 10:13

Imputed righteousness
Christ became sin for us

No requirements or commitments for becoming righteous

Little or no emphasis on indwelling or abiding in Christ

Righteousness is optional

Little or no emphasis on relationship to the Lord

No emphasis on repentance

SCRIPTURES AND DISCUSSION TO FOLLOW

### LORDSHIP EVANGELISM
### ROMANS ROAD TO SALVATION PLUS

I. I believe that You, Jesus, are the Son of God and that God raised You from the dead to provide salvation for me. I am attracted to You, Your truth and light and I purpose to allow Your Spirit to guide my life. John 3:16, 21, Ro. 10:9

II. I ask you, Lord, to come into my life and I wholeheartedly welcome You to come in as Lord and Master of my life. Rev. 3:20, Ro. 1:21, Ro. 10:13, Pslm. 145:18-20, Ro. 8:9, 1 Jo. 4:15

III. I will learn of Your ways from the Bible and will do my utmost to obey your teachings. Matt. 28:19-20, Pslm 119:11, 97-104

IV. I am sorry for my sins, confess them to you and in repentance, with Your help, turn from, forsake, and overcome them, and as quickly as possible begin to become the new creation You want me to be. Luke 13:3, 1 Jo. 5:1-5, 2 Cor. 5:17

V. With all the strength of my being, in compliance to Your #1 commandment, I will purpose to love you more and more, which will empower me to do Your will and to love and treat others as You desire. Matt. 22:36-37, John 14:23, 1 John 3:10

VI. I will grow in my personal relationship with You and serve You in an assembly of other like-spirited Believers that preach and live Your word. Heb. 10:22-25

Consequently they have no relationship with Jesus (which 90% of Americans admit on a survey). They have little or no obedience to His Word (Bible or direct promptings to their soul), and no "victory in Jesus". This results in their "religion not working for them" and they become spiritual drop-outs leaving the church or possibly staying in the church because of their social, business, or entertainment needs being met.

Stopping with easy believism (tritely believing and calling on the Lord for salvation) will not get us to the "heart condition" and the "truth" that will set us free! (John 8:31-32,36)

The good news to these souls is that with exposure to and embracing "Lordship" evangelism and discipleship scriptures, hard packed, rocky, and thorny "souls" can be broken up, tilled, watered, nourished and rendered productive becoming good souls yielding much fruit.

It is scripturally very reasonable that Lordship evangelism and discipling could yield up to an 80% or higher genuinely saved group of "followers" and only 20% or lower being lost.

Individuals, churches and any nation can possibly go beyond revival and have a spiritual awakening that has never been seen before by adding Lordship evangelism and scriptures, and commitments for salvation, coupled with intense consistent preaching and teaching focusing on the Lordship discipling scriptures.

It is imperative that the church make every possible effort driven and guided by the Lord to move the spiritual distribution of the congregation toward the spiritual Hot side of the Bell Curve.

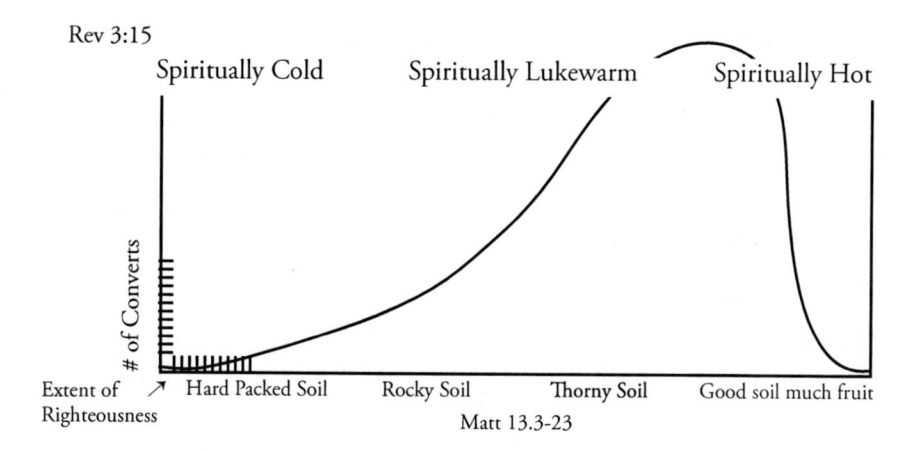

```
Rev 3:15
Spiritually Cold      Spiritually Lukewarm      Spiritually Hot
```

*(Chart: # of Converts vs. Extent of Righteousness — Hard Packed Soil, Rocky Soil, Thorny Soil, Good soil much fruit — Matt 13.3-23)*

This effect would be from a deliberate effort to affect the "population" in the Bell Curve from an undesirable to a desirable condition. Interestingly, in the statistical world, this would be called "skewing the population" to the <u>RIGHT</u>. Lordship Christianity evangelism and discipling can do this!

How can this be done?

You have already seen much on this subject. The Lordship evangelism and discipling scriptures give much attention and insights to the solutions.

Let's explore a real time example of this process working by showing a letter segment from a woman writing an appreciation letter to a wonderful organization that distributes Bibles to people in countries "closed" to Christianity:

> A young teacher from a closed nation writes, "All my life I got a very bad feeling against Christ and Christian people and of course against the Bible ... But after I read the Bible, I can say very surely that I love Christ ... I want to believe in him so much and forever."

This letter speaks volumes about the negative consequences of easy believism. This lady was very turned off to Christianity and the Bible because what she had heard about or observed in some of

Christ's "followers". When she explored the Bible herself, and most likely OBSERVING AND EMBRACING MANY SCRIPTURES OMITTED OR MISINTERPRETED BY EASY BELIEVISM, the negative impressions became dim and fell away and she began to love the Lord and delighted in His high holy standards and in Christianity.

Easy believism Christianity grants permission for new and old believers to continue to grope in their darkness even for a lifetime and still be acceptably within God's will regarding their salvation. They can stay an angry person, be high minded, prideful, exclusionary in their relationships, envious, bitter, unloving, unforgiving, inflexible, immoral, harsh, lustful, selfish, extremely abusive, divisive, insensitive, obsessed with winning no matter what the cost or who gets hurt, over-delighting and indulgent in all other sorts of worldliness. They can apparently be a church member and display the "last days" qualities described by Paul in II Timothy 3:1-7 (especially note 5 and 7).

"Christians" remaining in darkness are "enemies of the cross" in a sense. Some of the peoples of the world hate Christianity because the "bad" hate the goodness of the good. However, many people (both good and bad) hate Christians who are supposed to be good but grope around in darkness as bad or worse than those who reject the Lord.

GENUINE CHRISTIANITY IS THE MOST MARVELOUS POSITIVE UNPARALLELED, BENEFICIAL, BLESSED MESSAGE ON THE PLANET. The difficulties genuine Christianity has had through the ages, have been that the masses of the religiously inclined have promoted the messages and messengers who allowed them, after all the preaching and teaching dust has settled, to do what they want to do - doing what's right in their own eyes and desires, and then going to heaven. This has evolved through a slow moving Satan-driven self-serving process of embracing certain scriptures, and ignoring and/or misinterpreting others. For example:

| Embracing | Ignoring or Misinterpreting |
|---|---|
| John 3:16 | John 3:17-21 |
| Eph. 2:8,9 | Eph. 10 |
| 1 Cor. 3:13-15 | 1 Cor. 3:16-17 |
| 1 John 1:9 | 1 John 1:5-7, 2:3-6 |
| Ro. 4:3,6,24 | 2 Thess. 2:10-11 |
| Ro. 8:28 | 1 John 2:29 |
|  | Ro. 6:1-2,6,14,18 |
|  | John 14:21 |
| Other "easy believism" scriptures | Other Lordship scriptures |

Those professing that they have accepted the message must get on the fast track to overcoming their badness for the following four main reasons:

* They <u>overcome their worldliness</u> with its badness or there are strong indications that they are not true believers (born of God) I John 5:1-5 (below)

* If they do not, they will indulge in and/or reproduce their badness in their families with a strong possibility of destroying them.

* Many who observe the badness of Christians reject Christ as did the lady who wrote the above (the young teacher who read the Bible herself).

* Much of the world has "had it" with all the absence of the Lord's "light and salt" in His "followers" and are becoming very intent to trample Christianity asunder. (Matt. 5:13-16) Of course there are other motives to do the same thing.

Lordship Christianity scriptures slam the door shut on the current prevailing notion that "followers" of the Lord have an option as to whether or not they are to become righteous.

"Love" is the primary ingredient in all this whole matter. When we intensely love our spouse, our children, our parents, our relatives, our closest friend, we are highly motivated to comply or "obey" or fulfill their spoken requests and even their unspoken desires. This was especially dramatically evident when we first fell in love with our chosen marriage partner (or junior high or high school sweetheart). We would do <u>anything</u> to promote winning and keeping their heart and promote the relationship. (Life is at its best when we keep this up with our spouse and children.)

When we intensely love the Lord, we are likewise highly motivated to promote a relationship with Him by obeying His commands and other teachings. (John 14:21).

When just "doing" what our Lord says comes from merely learning or hearing a command and doing it "without Him" falls short, it is empty and void of what He wants. He wants us to do it in, through, and with His love in us. We do it right and can keep doing it right when it comes from genuine compliance to His #1 and #2 commands.

## Matthew 22:36-39

> Master, which is the great commandment in the law? [37] Jesus said unto him, Thou shalt love the Lord thy God with all thy heart, and with all thy soul, and with all thy mind. [38] This is the first and great commandment. [39] And the second is like unto it, Thou shalt love thy neighbour as thyself.

## 1 John 3:10

> In this the children of God are manifest, and the children of the devil: <u>whosoever doeth not righteousness is not of God</u>, neither he that loveth not his brother.

## 1 John 5:1-5

> Whosoever believeth that Jesus is the Christ is born of God: and every one that loveth him that begat loveth him also that is begotten of him. [2] By this we know that we love the children of God, <u>when we love God, and keep his commandments</u>. [3] For this is the love of God, that <u>we keep his commandments: and his commandments are not grievous. (too hard) [4] For whatsoever is born of God overcometh the world</u>: and this is the victory that overcometh the world, even our faith. [5] <u>Who is he that overcometh the world, but he that believeth that Jesus is the Son of God?</u>

As we see in 1 John 5:1-5, obeying His righteous commands and overcoming our natural worldliness (sin and disobedience) is only doable when we are true believers – that Jesus together with God is God and if He <u>is</u> God, He is <u>our</u> God (king, sovereign authority, master) and we love Him and delight in Him indwelling us and all the power and victory over sinning this gives us.

## John 15:5

> I am the vine, ye are the branches: He that abideth in me, and I in him, the same bringeth forth much fruit: for without me ye can do nothing.

Jesus gives us some proper motivation to love Him when we read and study just one of the rewards for repenting and overcoming after having "lost our first love" of Him.

## Rev. 2:4-5 (Church of Ephesus).

> Nevertheless I have somewhat against thee, because thou hast left thy first love. [5] Remember therefore from whence thou art fallen, and repent, and do the first works; or else I will come unto thee quickly, and will remove thy candlestick out of his place, except thou repent.

## Rev. 2:7

He that hath an ear, let him hear what the Spirit saith unto the churches; <u>To him that overcometh will I give to eat of the tree of life, which is in the midst of the paradise of God.</u>

Of great concern are the scriptures that closely relate going to Heaven with doing the Lord's will.

## Matthew 7:21

Not every one that saith unto me, Lord, Lord, shall enter into the kingdom of heaven; but he that doeth the will of my Father which is in heaven.

## 1 John 2:17

And the world passeth away, and the lust thereof: but he that doeth the will of God abideth for ever.

Doing His will is not just compliance in a few major factors of our lives. With Him indwelling us, we will have a grateful, repentant, learner's heart and a teachable spirit and will <u>do</u> His teachings in many, many areas. (Matt. 7:21-23, Luke 6:46, John 10:26-28) We must not just casually <u>know</u> the Lord. <u>We glorify Him as the personal Lord and Master of our lives.</u> If we do not do this, our lives will be an endless godless cascade of bad decisions and behavior that comes from foolish thinking.

## Romans 1:21-22

Because that, when they knew God, they glorified him not as God, neither were thankful; but became vain in their imaginations, and their foolish heart was darkened. [22] Professing themselves to be wise, they became fools,

Without glorifying the Lord as our Lord and indwelling Master we will be powerless against the world, flesh and the devil. With His power, believers can and will <u>overcome</u> these things. From our intense love of Him and desire to please Him, we possess much power to add to the power of His indwelling us and we will do what He says. We have already seen what John 5:1-5 says on the matter. Let's look at some reinforcements: John 15:4-5, 1 John 4:15, 2:29, 3:5,6,9,10, Ro. 8: 9, Ro. 6:14,18.

With Jesus Christ indwelling us and with His power, His commands (must do's) will not be burdensome and become our <u>want to's</u> and <u>can do's</u> and <u>will do's</u> as we repent and overcome our unrighteousness and start doing His righteousness.

## 1 John 2:3-6

> And hereby we do know that we know him, if we keep his commandments. [4] He that saith, I know him, and keepeth not his commandments, is a liar, and the truth is not in him. [5] But whoso keepeth his word, in him verily is the love of God perfected: hereby know we that we are in him. [6] He that saith he abideth in him ought himself also so to walk, even as he walked.

<u>Salvation, worship and a relationship</u> with the Lord that "works" is laced with unusual, amazing or supernatural happenings. The new or old Lordship "convert" can be frequented with answered prayer, special guidance, experience special comfort, give special comfort, have unusual calmness, self-control, supernatural ability to love or do things beyond their natural talents or capabilities. Selfishness, anger, or bitterness can fall away. Avoiding temptation, repentance, forgiveness and reconciliation become possible and evident. Wisdom directly from the Lord from promptings through prayer or through the Bible strengthens and blesses much of what they do, including their marriage and ability to rear successful Lordship children. They develop the fruit of the Spirit.

## Galatians 5:22-23

> But the fruit of the Spirit is love, joy, peace, longsuffering, gentleness, goodness, faith, [23] Meekness, temperance: against such there is no law.

As genuine followers of the Lord, we can and will truly <u>add righteous qualities to our belief and faith</u> insuring our reception into the eternal kingdom of God and be free from the destruction Peter mentions in 2 Peter and Jesus mentions in Matt. 7 and Luke 13.

Don Z. Weldon

## 2 Peter 3:14-16

Wherefore, beloved, seeing that ye look for such things, be diligent that ye may be found of him in peace, without spot, and blameless. [15] And account that the longsuffering of our Lord is salvation; even as our beloved brother Paul also according to the wisdom given unto him hath written unto you; [16] As also in all his epistles, speaking in them of these things; in which are some things hard to be understood, which they that are unlearned and unstable wrest, as they do also the other scriptures, unto their own destruction.

## 2 Peter 1:3-11

According as his divine power hath given unto us all things that pertain unto life and godliness, through the knowledge of him that hath called us to glory and virtue: [4] Whereby are given unto us exceeding great and precious promises: that by these ye might be partakers of the divine nature, having escaped the corruption that is in the world through lust. [5] And beside this, giving all diligence, <u>ADD TO YOUR FAITH</u> virtue; and to virtue knowledge; [6] And to knowledge temperance; and to temperance patience; and to patience godliness; [7] And to godliness brotherly kindness; and to brotherly kindness charity. [8] For if these things be in you, and abound, they make you that ye shall neither be barren nor unfruitful in the knowledge of our Lord Jesus Christ. [9] But he that lacketh these things is blind, and cannot see afar off, and <u>hath forgotten that he was purged from his old sins</u>. [10] Wherefore the rather, brethren, give diligence to <u>make your calling and election sure</u>: for if ye do these things, ye shall never fall: [11] <u>For so an entrance shall be ministered unto you abundantly into the everlasting kingdom of our Lord and Saviour Jesus Christ.</u>

## Matthew 7:21-23

Not every one that saith unto me, Lord, Lord, shall enter into the kingdom of heaven; but he that doeth the will of my Father which is in heaven. [22] Many will say to me in that day, Lord, Lord, have we not prophesied in thy name? and in thy name have cast out devils? and in thy name done many wonderful works? [23] And then will I profess unto them, I never knew you: depart from me, ye that work iniquity.

## Luke 13:23-24

Then said one unto him, Lord, are there few that be saved? And he said unto them,

[24] Strive to enter in at the strait gate: for many, I say unto you, will seek to enter in, and shall not be able.

## Luke 13:27-28

But he shall say, I tell you, I know you not whence ye are; depart from me, all ye workers of iniquity. [28] There shall be weeping and gnashing of teeth, when ye shall see Abraham, and Isaac, and Jacob, and all the prophets, in the kingdom of God, and you yourselves thrust out.

We will not become sinless, but we will progressively sin less and less after we truly become saved and grow in a relationship with Him and respond appropriately to His Word. (1 John 1:8,10, 3:9-10) We can conquer sins of omission and sins of commission. Luke 13:3, Gal. 5:24, Ro. 6:18, 8:1.

Observe the parallels in these scriptures of <u>condemned</u> "professed believers" of the Lord and <u>non-condemned</u> believers who live in His truth and light. John 3:18-21, 1 John 1:5-7.

Being non-condemned, we are attracted to Jesus' "truth and light", and what we become and do reflects His Spirit in us. Our spirit and His Spirit unite and cooperate, which affects our deeds and how we live our lives. (Look up "wrought" in the original language regarding John 3:21). Read and meditate on John 3:16-21 over and over until you see this. Your conclusion could affect your <u>forever</u>.

In all this scriptural emphasis of our Lord requiring us to develop righteousness after we become a "believer" or a Christian, we have to be very careful not to over focus on doing what Jesus says and neglect creating and maintaining a close personal intimate communicative love relationship with Him.  <u>If our obedience to His commands is done through our decisions and our strength, without Him and His will specifically directing all facets of the obediences, we will miss His power, His perfect will, and displease Him.  In a sense, the act of obedience can become Pharisaical in nature and fall short or fail</u>.

Each church member must keep focused that no matter how many times you win or lose, how many friends you have and who they are, how many church jobs you have done, how strong or weak your portfolio or extent of your possessions, whether you have been famed or fowled, how strong or weak your influence; all these are issues that in eternity are insignificant.  Life on earth is a minute dress rehearsal and really has only one thing that is really important to each individual – did we, through a close relationship, establish <u>the</u> Lord as <u>our</u> Lord, Master, and Supreme Authority and help <u>ours</u> and <u>others</u> do likewise.

Many believers have a confused notion about living their lives by avoiding good deeds because it might appear they are working for their salvation.  We are taught we are "free from the law" – which to many means we can disregard doing His Holy ways and this includes disobeying the Ten Commandments, the Sermon on the Mount and the rest of the Bible.  In error, we feel that the "imputed" righteousness from Jesus at conversion time covers everything and we do not need to live and act as righteous people after becoming saved.  Many fall into thinking God is in control of everything so therefore whatever we do must be from His control.  This is all the righteousness we need.  After we "believe" and "call on the Lord" to be saved, whatever God makes or allows us to do, that is His will and is all that is required of us and it will turn out for good.  <u>It will turn out good only if we love Him and are in or will get into His will</u> (Ro. 8:28, John 14:21, Matt. 7:21).

With all these confused notions, with ninety percent of our population admitting they have no personal relationship with Jesus, and with so little understanding of spiritual warfare, (see Eph. 6:10-18) there is no wonder why believers so offensively misbehave, and are so defeated and drop out spiritually because their religion is "not working" for them.

* Easy believism can and has obviously led to the salvation of many people if they grew into Lordship Christianity.

* Lordship Christianity is not something new; it is returning to something as old as the Bible teachings.

* In these dangerous times, with all the destructive forces battling for the embracing and allegiance of our minds - the greatest, most precious, most stabilizing earthly asset a husband, wife, child, parent or grandparent can have is a Lordship Christian husband, wife, child, parent or grandparent!

* The horrible, unbelievable and unacceptable extent of marital affairs and breakups of church members is one of the greatest indicators of the failings of easy believism. The greatest, surest and quickest route to marital reconciliation, rejuvenation and maintenance is Lordship Christianity with all its emphasis on the presence and power of the indwelling Lord. With His Spirit enabling the power of scriptural principles on marriage, repentance and overcoming, claiming the promises, self-control, peace, joy, God's grace, love, overpowering Satan's involvement, forgiveness, obedience to the Lord, "hearing" the Lord's voice, becoming a new creation, and <u>many</u> other scriptures to come alive and well in the individuals and marriage relationship, healing is assured! This can even be done without but preferably with a strong Lordship Christian counselor.

* Easy believism is incompatible with and <u>exclusive</u> of Lordship. Lordship Christianity is <u>inclusive</u> of easy believism in that it takes it to a whole new level!

* Easy believism is reinforced in churches which have much worldly entertainment of the senses. Isn't it quite possible that this contributes to the current statistic of losing 80% of our church youth who become "overcome by the world" after leaving the home and home church and become spiritual dropouts by age 26?

Lordship will grow a church and provide sustained long term "overcoming the world" for the members through edification of the spirit, koinonia (Holy Spirit prospered close interpersonal relationships), emphasis on conviction, repentance, genuine love of the Lord and others, relationship reconciliation, depending on the Lord's power, and strongly emphasizing the non-optional growing relationship with the Lord and the resultant obedience, righteousness and victory (Acts 36-47).

* Effective communication is the essential ingredient in successful relationships. Frequent, consistent, persistent prayer is an underpinning foundation, and catalyst in a "close" Lordship relationship with Jesus Christ. This should be done in a personal atmosphere of praise, thanksgiving and righteousness.

## 1 Thes. 5:16-22

Rejoice evermore. [17] PRAY WITHOUT CEASING. [18] In every thing give thanks: for this is the will of God in Christ Jesus concerning you. [19] Quench not the Spirit. [20] Despise not prophesyings. [21] Prove all things; hold fast that which is good. [22] Abstain from all appearance of evil.

## John 10:26-28

But ye believe not, because ye are not of my sheep, as I said unto you. [27] My sheep hear my voice, and I know them, and they follow me: [28] And I give unto them eternal life; and they shall never perish, neither shall any man pluck them out of my hand.

Prayer from a repentant, cleaned up, overcoming soul, is very much a part of "hearing His voice".

The astronomically important question comes up, and must be nailed down: "Will a cold or lukewarm believer or "Christian" go to Heaven?" Let's review some of the scriptures you have seen over and over in this material. (We have added a few.) You have heard the easy believism scriptures and answers to this question perhaps hundreds of times so we won't apologize for presenting the Lordship scriptures again. As you go through these, earnestly ask God to reveal the (His) truth to you. SCRIPTURALLY REASON WITH GOD'S HELP AS TO HOW CRITICAL THESE SCRIPTURES ARE AS PART OF YOUR "BELIEVING" AND "CALLING" ON THE LORD TO BE SAVED:

## Psalm 145:18-20

The Lord is nigh unto all them that call upon him, to all that <u>call upon him in truth</u>. [19] He will fulfil the desire of them that fear him: he also will hear their cry, and will save them. [20] The Lord preserveth all them that love him: but all the wicked will he destroy.

## 2 Peter 3:9

The Lord is not slack concerning his promise, as some men count slackness; but is longsuffering to us-ward, not willing that any should perish, but that all should come to repentance.

## Luke 13:3

I tell you, Nay: but, except ye repent, ye shall all likewise perish.

## Luke 24:47

And that repentance and remission of sins should be preached in his name among all nations, beginning at Jerusalem.

## Luke 6:46

And why call ye me, Lord, Lord, and do not the things which I say?

## Matthew 7:21-24

NOT EVERY ONE THAT SAITH UNTO ME, LORD, LORD, SHALL ENTER INTO THE KINGDOM OF HEAVEN; <u>BUT HE THAT DOETH THE WILL OF MY FATHER</u> which is in heaven. [22] Many will say to me in that day, Lord, Lord, have we not prophesied in thy name? and in thy name have cast out devils? and in thy name done many wonderful works? [23] And then will I profess unto them, <u>I never knew you: depart from me, ye that work iniquity</u>.

[24] <u>Therefore</u> whosoever heareth these sayings of mine, and doeth them, I will liken him unto a wise man, which built his house upon a rock:

## 2 Tim. 2:19

Nevertheless the foundation of God standeth sure, having this seal, THE LORD KNOWETH THEM THAT ARE HIS. <u>And, Let every one that nameth the name of Christ depart from iniquity.</u>

## Romans 6:1-2

What shall we say then? Shall we continue in sin, that grace may abound? [2] God forbid. How shall we, that are dead to sin, live any longer therein?

## Romans 6:6

Knowing this, that our old man is crucified with him, that the body of sin might be destroyed, that henceforth we should not serve sin.

## Romans 6:14

For sin shall not have dominion over you: for ye are not under the law, but under grace.

## Romans 6:18

Being then made free from sin, ye became the servants of righteousness.

## Romans 6:22

But now being made free from sin, and become servants to God, ye have your fruit unto holiness, and the end everlasting life.

## 1 Samuel 12:14-15

If ye will fear the Lord, and serve him, and obey his voice, and not rebel against the commandment of the Lord, then shall both ye and also the king that reigneth over you continue following the Lord your God: [15] But if ye will not obey the voice of the Lord, but rebel against the commandment of the Lord, then shall the hand of the Lord be against you, as it was against your fathers.

## Romans 8:1-2

There is therefore now no condemnation to them which are in Christ Jesus, who walk not after the flesh, but after the Spirit. [2] For the law of the Spirit of life in Christ Jesus hath made me free from the law of sin and death.

## Galatians 5:24

And they that are Christ's have crucified the flesh with the affections and lusts.

## Romans 8:7,9

Because the carnal mind is enmity against God: for it is not subject to the law of God, neither indeed can be. [9] But ye are not in the flesh, but in the Spirit, if so be that the Spirit of God dwell in you. <u>Now if any man have not the Spirit of Christ, he is none of his.</u>

## Galatians 5:21

Envyings, murders, drunkenness, revellings, and such like: of the which I tell you before, as I have also told you in time past, that they which do such things shall not inherit the kingdom of God.

## Matthew 13:41-43

The Son of man shall send forth his angels, and they shall gather out of his kingdom all things that offend, and them which do iniquity; [42] And shall cast them into a furnace of fire: there shall be wailing and gnashing of teeth. [43] Then shall the righteous shine forth as the sun in the kingdom of their Father. Who hath ears to hear, let him hear.

## Matthew 25:44-46

Then shall they also answer him, saying, Lord, when saw we thee an hungred, or athirst, or a stranger, or naked, or sick, or in prison, and did not minister unto thee? [45] Then shall he answer them, saying, Verily I say unto you, Inasmuch as ye did it not to one of the least of these, ye did it not to me. [46] AND THESE SHALL GO AWAY INTO EVERLASTING PUNISHMENT: BUT THE RIGHTEOUS INTO LIFE ETERNAL.

### James 1:22

But be ye doers of the word, and not hearers only, deceiving your own selves.

### James 2:17

Even so faith, if it hath not works, is dead, being alone.

### James 2:22

Seest thou how faith wrought with his works, and by works was faith made perfect?

### 1 John 5:5

WHO IS HE THAT OVERCOMETH THE WORLD, BUT HE THAT BELIEVETH THAT JESUS IS THE SON OF GOD?

### Romans 10:9-10

That if thou shalt confess with thy mouth the Lord Jesus, and shalt believe in thine heart that God hath raised him from the dead, thou shalt be saved. [10] <u>FOR WITH THE HEART MAN BELIEVETH UNTO RIGHTEOUSNESS</u>; and with the mouth confession is made unto salvation.

### Romans 10:2-3

For I bear them record that they have a zeal of God, but not according to knowledge. [3] For they being ignorant of God's righteousness, and going about to establish their own righteousness, have not submitted themselves unto the righteousness of God.

### 1 John 4:15

Whosoever shall confess that Jesus is the Son of God, God dwelleth in him, and he in God.

### 1 John 2:6

He that saith he abideth in him ought himself also so to walk, even as he walked.

### 1 John 3:10

In this the children of God are manifest, and the children of the devil: whosoever doeth not righteousness is not of God, neither he that loveth not his brother.

### 1 John 2:4

He that saith, I know him, and keepeth not his commandments, is a liar, and the truth is not in him.

### 1 John 2:29

If ye know that he is righteous, ye know that every one that doeth righteousness is born of him.

### Matthew 5:6

Blessed are they which do hunger and thirst after righteousness: for they shall be filled.

### Matthew 5:10

Blessed are they which are persecuted for righteousness' sake: for theirs is the kingdom of heaven.

### Matthew 28:19-20

Go ye therefore, and teach all nations, baptizing them in the name of the Father, and of the Son, and of the Holy Ghost: [20] TEACHING THEM TO OBSERVE ALL THINGS WHATSOEVER I HAVE COMMANDED YOU: and, lo, I am with you alway, even unto the end of the world. Amen.

### Rev. 3:1-3 (Spiritually <u>cold</u> church members of Sardis)

And unto the angel of the church in Sardis write; These things saith he that hath the seven Spirits of God, and the seven stars; I know thy works, that thou hast a name that thou livest, and art dead. [2] Be watchful, and strengthen the things which remain, that are ready to die: for I have not found thy works perfect before God. [3] Remember therefore how thou hast received and heard, and hold fast, and <u>repent</u>. If therefore thou shalt not watch, I will come on thee as a thief, and thou shalt not know what hour I will come upon thee.

## Rev. 3:5

<u>He that overcometh</u>, the same shall be clothed in white raiment; <u>and I will not blot out his name out of the book of life, but I will confess his name before my Father, and before his angels.</u>

## Rev. 3:15-17 (Spiritually <u>lukewarm</u> church members of Laodicea)

I know thy works, that thou art neither cold nor hot: I would thou wert cold or hot. [16] So then because thou art lukewarm, and neither cold nor hot, I will spue thee out of my mouth. [17] Because thou sayest, I am rich, and increased with goods, and have need of nothing; and knowest not that thou art wretched, and miserable, and poor, and blind, and naked:

## Rev. 3:19-21

As many as I love, I rebuke and chasten: be zealous therefore, and <u>repent</u>. [20] Behold, I stand at the door, and knock: if any man hear my voice, and open the door, I will come in to him, and will sup with him, and he with me. [21] <u>To him that overcometh will I grant to sit with me in my throne, even as I also overcame, and am set down with my Father in his throne.</u>

## Luke 13:23-24

Then said one unto him, Lord, are there few that be saved? And he said unto them,   [24] Strive to enter in at the strait gate: for many, I say unto you, will seek to enter in, and shall not be able.

## Luke 13:27-28

But he shall say, I tell you, I know you not whence ye are; depart from me, all ye workers of iniquity. [28] There shall be weeping and gnashing of teeth, when ye shall see Abraham, and Isaac, and Jacob, and all the prophets, in the kingdom of God, and you yourselves thrust out.

## John 8:12

Then spake Jesus again unto them, saying, <u>I am the light of the world: he that followeth me shall not walk in darkness, but shall have the light of life.</u>

## John 14:21

He that hath my commandments, and keepeth them, he it is that loveth me: and he that loveth me shall be loved of my Father, and I will love him, and will manifest myself to him.

## John 14:23

Jesus answered and said unto him, If a man love me, he will keep my words: and my Father will love him, and we will come unto him, and make our abode with him.

## 2 Thes. 2:10-12

And with all deceivableness of unrighteousness in them that perish; because they received not the love of the truth, that they might be saved. [11] And for this cause God shall send them strong delusion, that they should believe a lie: [12] That they all might be damned who believed not the truth, but had pleasure in unrighteousness.

## Titus 1:16

They profess that they know God; but in works they deny him, being abominable, and disobedient, and unto every good work reprobate.

## Romans 1:21

Because that, when they knew God, THEY GLORIFIED HIM NOT AS GOD, neither were thankful; but became vain in their imaginations, and their foolish heart was darkened.

## 2 Cor. 5:17

Therefore if any man be in Christ, he is a new creature: old things are passed away; behold, all things are become new.

## 1 Cor. 2:9

But as it is written, Eye hath not seen, nor ear heard, neither have entered into the heart of man, the things which God hath prepared for them that love him.

## 2 Chron. 16:9

For the eyes of the Lord run to and fro throughout the whole earth, to shew himself strong in the behalf of them whose heart is perfect toward him. Herein thou hast done foolishly: therefore from henceforth thou shalt have wars. (*within ourselves, family, church, nation*)

## Eccles. 12:13-14

Let us hear the conclusion of the whole matter: FEAR GOD, AND KEEP HIS COMMANDMENTS: FOR THIS IS THE WHOLE DUTY OF MAN. [14] For God shall bring every work into judgment, with every secret thing, whether it be good, or whether it be evil.

Enabling the Lord (God the Father, Son and Holy Spirit) to become your personal Lord and Master (compliance to His commands and wishes) becomes PARAMOUNT in these scriptures. ANY CONCLUSION OTHER THAN THIS SEEMS THAT IT COULD BE AN EXTREMELY RISKY GAMBLE WHEN YOUR (AND YOUR'S) FOREVER AND FOREVER ETERNITY IS AT STAKE!

If you still feel you can casually say or pray you "believe" or really believe but go through the act of <u>calling</u> on the Lord without making absolutely sure you are really willing and able to let <u>Him</u> and <u>His ways</u> come into your heart and life enabling Him to be your Lord, Master and "Controller", eliminating much of your willful, habitual, or defiant favorite sins, you are doing a very "fearful thing" !

## Matthew 5:20

> For I say unto you, That except your righteousness shall exceed the righteousness of the scribes and Pharisees, ye shall in no case enter into the kingdom of heaven.

Comparing ourselves to a Pharisee in this scripture is of minor importance. What is important is the obvious emphasis of righteousness into its proper place regarding salvation.

The continual willful, habitual, and/or defiant indulgence in your favorite sins and other unrighteousness and non-compliance to the Lord's high and holy standards after you become saved is a "mockery" to Him and His blood sacrifice and salvation provisions.

## Luke 10:25-28

> And, behold, a certain lawyer stood up, and tempted him, saying, Master, what shall I do to INHERIT ETERNAL LIFE? [26] He said unto him, What is written in the law? how readest thou? [27] And he answering said, Thou shalt LOVE THE LORD THY GOD WITH ALL THY HEART, and with all thy soul, and with all thy strength, and with all thy mind; AND THY NEIGHBOUR AS THYSELF. [28] And he said unto him, Thou hast answered right: this do, and thou shalt live.

RIGHTEOUS LIVING IS NOT A REQUIREMENT TO ATTAIN HEAVEN, BUT A BELIEVING PERSONAL LOVE/OBEDIENCE ABIDING RELATIONSHIP WITH OUR LORD IS A REQUIREMENT – WHICH WILL RESULT IN RIGHTEOUS LIVING!

With Lordship Christianity, we can and will become what God requires of any nation – a land with believing individuals who choose righteousness – reproducing righteous generations in strong, righteous homes.

The Lordship Christianity scriptures are marvelous absolute necessities to church leadership success as far as properly motivating the congregation to truly listen, and learn, repent and overcome in compliance to what is being taught from the Lord's Word.

Attaining wonderful heaven and avoiding awful hell are two of the primary motivations for becoming a Christian. When people see or hear so much scripture that heaven is "elusive" to those in cold and lukewarm unrighteous spiritual conditions, which reveals an absence of the transformation power of a personal abiding relationship with Jesus Christ, many will be highly motivated to "repent and overcome", seek an indwelling relationship with Jesus and "walk in righteousness" as He walked. What a boon to spiritual leaders to lead us with the Bible and prayer to "higher ground"!

What an incredible positive impact this would have on the current extent of church member divorces and on the ability of Christian homes to pass on genuine Lordship Christianity to future generations! What else could we do that would more (1) inevitably inspire the Lord to provide us with a sustained God blessed and protected America and (2) increase the numbers of church members genuinely becoming saved.

**Please allow us to get up close and personal on this salvation issue.**

If you are comfortable with easy believism and feel you have "grown in the Lord" since your "conversion", the issue is worthy of some serious eternity impacting soul searching. Did you grow in just becoming better <u>acquainted</u> with Him and His Word, or did you internalize Him and His ways such that you are enabled to repent, overcome, and obey His teachings "glorifying" Him as your controlling Master?

The summation of all this material is that our Lord came to earth not just so you could simply believe in Him and call on Him to save you and forgive your sins and save you from hell, all the while giving you slack to helplessly, hopelessly continue groping in godlessness, defeat, sin and darkness.

He came also to motivate and empower you to become a new creation when you become HIS! He loves you! However, He loves others in your life too! When you ignore, neglect, "embarrass", abuse (sin against) Him and His Holy ways and ignore, abuse, harm, neglect, high mindedly exclude (sin against) <u>others</u> that He loves, you are sinning against Him and out of compliance with HIS ways and will. (example Matt. 25:31-46, John 21:17)

If your believing on Him has led to enabling you to repent and overcome selfish worldliness in your life, you are fulfilling the purpose for your "believing in Him" as <u>the</u> Lord (which makes Him <u>your</u> LORD, savior and sovereign authority) bringing much righteousness into your life.

## 1 John 1:8

If we say that we have no sin, we deceive ourselves, and the truth is not in us.

## 1 John 3:5-10

And ye know that he was manifested (*appeared – original language*) to take away our sins; and in him is no sin. [6] Whosoever abideth in him sinneth not: whosoever sinneth hath not seen him, neither known him. [7] Little children, let no man deceive you: he that doeth righteousness is righteous, even as he is righteous. [8] He that committeth sin is of the devil; for the devil sinneth from the beginning. For this purpose the Son of God was manifested (*appeared*), that he might destroy the works of the devil. [9] Whosoever is born of God doth not commit sin; for his seed remaineth in him: and he cannot sin, because he is born of God. [10] In this the children of God are manifest, and the children of the devil: <u>whosoever doeth not righteousness is not of God, neither he that loveth not his brother</u>.

## Romans 6:18

Being then made free from sin, ye became the servants of righteousness.

If your "salvation" has no inclusion of our Lord's number one and number two "love" commands (and all that involves) and you continue to add so much "I" in to staying the lord of your own life, not only running, but <u>ruIning</u> your life, and many others you touch, you are precariously in a condition of being told to "depart from Me."

With the Lordship scriptures, which must no longer be ignored, included into your salvation and life, you and your family will gain many things on earth and everything in heaven. If you do not go further into true Christianity and let your "easy believism" become Lordship Christianity, you and your family can lose everything on

*Don Z. Weldon*

earth and in heaven. You can even bring some hell to earth for your family and others.

From an eternal perspective, with Lordship Christianity, you have everything to gain, nothing to lose.

From all the scriptures and principles, hopefully you have determined whether or not you are 100% sure of your salvation and will go to heaven!

If you would like to insure becoming a Lordship Christian, at this time, return to the "What About You and Your Loved Ones?" section on pages 25-31.

Perhaps you want to take some time to think and pray about this. We realize that it can be extremely difficult to relearn adding these Lordship scriptures to your faith. Please try harder than anything you've done before. Maybe take off for a week or month and reread and study this book, praying with all your heart, asking the Lord (God the Father, God the Son, and God the Holy Spirit) what He wants you to do!

"All things are possible with Almighty God!"